JAGUAR
Marketing the Marque

OTHER BOOKS BY NIGEL THORLEY:

You & Your Jaguar XK8
Jaguar Mark 1 & 2: Haynes Great Cars Series
You & Your Jaguar XJS (2nd Edition)
Jaguar E-type: Haynes Great Cars Series
Jaguar: All the cars
You & Your Jaguar XJ40
Jaguar XK: Haynes Great Cars Series

JAGUAR
Marketing the Marque

THE HISTORY OF JAGUAR SEEN THROUGH ITS ADVERTISING, BROCHURES AND CATALOGUES

Nigel Thorley

Haynes Publishing

© Haynes Publishing 2006

Nigel Thorley has asserted his right to be identified as the author of this work.

First published in 2006

A catalogue record for this book is available from the British Library

ISBN 978 1 84425 331 9

Library of Congress catalog card no. 2006924149

Published by
Haynes Publishing,
Sparkford, Yeovil,
Somerset BA22 7JJ, UK

Tel: 01963 442030
Fax: 01963 440001
Int. tel: +44 1963 442030
Int. fax: +44 1963 440001
E-mail: sales@haynes.co.uk
Website: www.haynes.co.uk

Haynes North America, Inc.,
861 Lawrence Drive, Newbury Park,
California 91320, USA

Designed by Helen McTeer
(helenmcteer@tiscali.co.uk)

Printed and bound in England by
J. H. Haynes & Co. Ltd, Sparkford

Contents

Acknowledgements

This is an entirely new type of publication on motoring heritage, and one that required a great deal of thought. I was lucky enough to have a large collection of material to work from, some of which is featured herein, but apart from this I honestly could not have completed this project without the tremendous help of a very dear friend and fellow Jaguar enthusiast and collector, Andrew Swift.

Andrew is well known as a dealer in motoring memorabilia, particularly brochures, books and marketing material, and his own personal collection is just incredible. Being a Jaguar enthusiast himself he also has an extensive background knowledge of such material, and his help was invaluable in the preparation of this book. My sincere thanks go to him.

As usual, the work involved in putting this book together has taken time and hard work – plus, in this particular case, a great deal of space! Having thousands of brochures and items of allied material spread around one's house for months on end is not a recipe for domestic bliss, so I am grateful to my wife Pauline for putting up with it all; at least now most of the material is back in the loft or garage!

Thanks also to Haynes, and in particular Mark Hughes, for their continued support and understanding of the importance of publishing books about unique aspects of Jaguar and other marques.

Finally, thank you for buying and reading this publication. I hope you enjoy it.

Nigel Thorley
South Yorkshire, November 2006

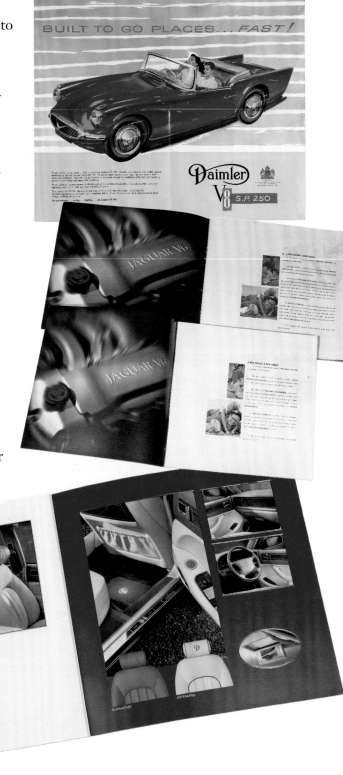

Introduction

The motor car has dominated the 20th and 21st centuries, and since the 1950s there can hardly have been a schoolboy who didn't go to great pains to acquire brochures about the cars they most 'fancied'. By cajoling dads or elder brothers to get the prized brochure from a local car dealer, by utilising 'pester power' to bully them into visiting the annual motor show, or by gingerly writing to the manufacturers for the latest information on particular models – by fair means or foul, it was vital to build up one's collection of brochures on the 'best' cars around. In more recent times, there has been a growth in the number of collectors (of all ages) of such material, sometimes themed, sometimes merely randomly accumulated.

There is, however, a more serious aspect to car brochures as a means of promotion, even an 'invitation to treat' as the legal term implies, as an important tool used by manufacturers to entice, encourage interest and motivate aspiration for their products. Manufacturers have used many different approaches to this end, none more so than Jaguar, variously appealing to emotion, to contemporary fashion or, occasionally, even to budgetary considerations! The marketing gurus also chose, from time to time, to concentrate on specific issues they felt important to prospective customers, from performance and mechanical attributes, to luxury appointments, lifestyle, or benefits over the competition; whatever it took to create a feeling of well-being by association with a particular car.

Even Jaguar have occasionally made somewhat dubious claims for their cars, or used the benefit of 'artistic licence' in brochure imagery to make people want their cars, which make for interesting reading now to anyone with even a passing interest in Jaguars. Like many other manufacturers they have been at the mercy of copywriters who occasionally got carried away with lavish statements. Manufacturers created clichés to put across a strong, memorable, message, invaluable in establishing the attributes of the marque – who, amongst Jaguar enthusiasts, cannot empathise with the slogan 'Grace…Space…and Pace', for example?

Jaguar have produced literally thousands of brochures on their models over the years, and the design, execution and production of these has cost many, many thousands of pounds. Yet despite its significance in its own right, this material was – and in the majority of cases still is – given away freely, as promotional tools in the hard world of car selling.

It is not the intention of this publication to provide a detailed historical review of every brochure produced by Jaguar, or even to look at the many varieties, rarities or unique features of brochures produced for global or specific markets. There are just too many to cover in such detail. It is, however, my intention to cover the different styles and approaches that the company (and their agents) have taken over the years to capture their market share: to identify changes in philosophy and ethos according to a moment in time or specific model, even the changes in attitude according to the importance new models played in the future of the company at a particular time.

The move from over-the-top, extravagantly produced 'books' for some models at one extreme, to simple single-sheet, black-and-white leaflets for others; the need to minimise paper usage after the Second World War; and the current trend of using enhanced digitised imagery and CDs, are just some of the many fascinating aspects of Jaguar marketing that the reader will find explored in the pages of this book.

Strategy by design

The reputation of a brand like Jaguar took years to establish, and like other manufacturers the company knew early on how vital marketing and promotion were. When one considers that the name 'Jaguar' didn't appear on the motoring scene until the mid-1930s, when it had to establish itself amongst the hierarchy of marques such as Alvis, Daimler, Humber, Riley, Rover, and even Bentley, the company's existence is not only a tribute to the cars they produced but also to the marketing strategy that helped achieve that success. Looking back now, it is significant that apart from Bentley the only one of these marques to survive is Jaguar (which includes Daimler).

As most people know, Jaguar has its origins in Blackpool, Lancashire, in 1922, when the original business – the Swallow Sidecar Company – produced motorcycle sidecars under the 'Swallow' name. Within just four years the business was fitting specialist bodies to contemporary motor cars like Austins.

Even in those days Swallow realised the importance of marketing material to help sell their products and establish the 'brand'. Comprehensive single- and two-colour fold-out brochures were produced covering the sidecar range, with detailed specifications and quality drawings of the vehicles, in one case even depicting accompanying motorcycles, riders and their passengers for maximum effect.

It was also during this early period that two important elements of brochure content took shape – a brand logo and the inevitable slogan. In Swallow's case they opted for a stylised swallow bird for their logo, while their initial slogan was 'Sidecars for the Connoisseur', later to become 'Coachwork for the Connoisseur'.

It is likely that the first Swallow brochure to feature cars didn't appear until after the company moved from Blackpool to Foleshill in Coventry c1928, initial car advertising being helped along by the Henlys organisation, then distributors for the Swallow-bodied Austins. The first car brochure epitomised the 'upwardly mobile' move the company and its customers were to take, incorporating highly detailed full colour prints from paintings of the individual models, set against idyllic backgrounds of coast

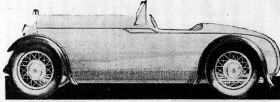

LEFT *'The world's most beautiful coachwork'. An example of early advertising for Swallow-bodied cars promoted and paid for by the Henlys organisation, hence the prominence of their name instead of Swallow. Reproduced from The Autocar of 24 April 1931.*

FAR LEFT *A good example of contemporary advertising by one of Swallow's coachbuilding competitors in the 1920s–30s, in this case featuring the Wolseley marque. Note the use of colour for the advertisement and for the vehicles; Swallow were taking ideas from such other specialists, though not emphasising them so strongly. Even at that time Swallow were 'pitching' on price – note the slight reduction of £5 for the Swallow Hornet in the advertisement (left), compared to the Eustace car here. Reproduced from The Autocar of 24 April 1931.*

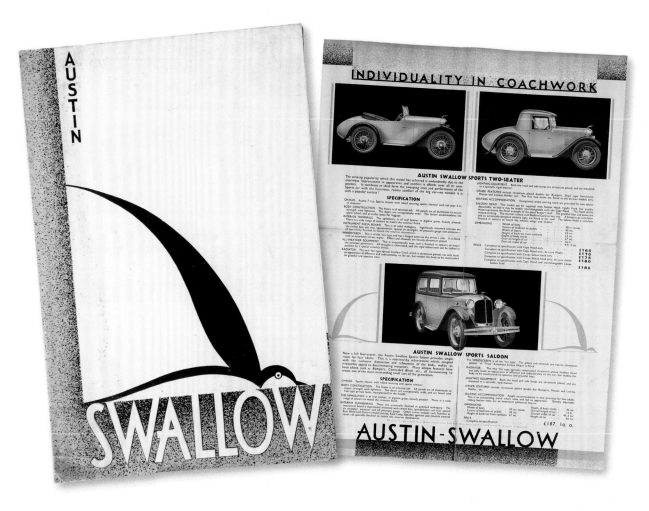

ABOVE *Typical of the Swallow brochures of the period, two-colour printing kept the cost down, as did drawings instead of expensive photography. Forming an impressive four-fold leaflet, this type of material was very informative even down to prices, colour schemes, and an optional extras list. The same approach continued into the SS era for the cheaper end of promotional material.*

and countryside. During these early days in Coventry the company not only produced individual brochures for the various marques bodied by Swallow but also the first 'range' brochures, featuring all the models and sometimes including sidecars as well.

Swallow to SS

From 1931 the company diversified into the design and assembly of its own cars, although using mechanical components from the Standard Motor Company. These cars were branded SS and initially were featured in other range brochures incorporating the remaining Swallow-bodied cars and the sidecars as well. Later, however, highlighting their increasing importance for the company, the SS models benefited from their own brochures with sidecars featured separately.

Throughout the 1930s, coinciding with an increase in SS car production and model range, the brochures were expanded and improved. A trend emerged – that most manufacturers follow

even to this day – of producing two versions of printed material, one simple in content, mostly single-page and cheap to produce for the mass market, and the other a quality production intended for serious potential buyers.

It is a tribute to the then company marketing and publicity expert, Ernest Rankin, that such a small company producing few cars could publish such interesting and ultimately expensive material. His attention to detail both in the content and production of these brochures continued for many years until his retirement in the 1960s.

The early days of Jaguar

Fuelled by the success of the SS models and his ambition to become a major car producer, William Lyons moved forward with a greater emphasis on car production and indeed a new concept of luxury transport. The Jaguar name now appeared for the first time – not as a brand, but merely the model designation for a new saloon: the SS Jaguar 2¹/2-litre.

This development saw the demise of Swallow-bodied cars and most of the other SS models. Swallow sidecar marketing material also took a back seat and, of course, with the outbreak of the Second World War all attention was turned to the war effort. Car production was eventually shut down for the duration of hostilities.

Post-war emphasis

After the war SS, like the rest of British industry, had to get back into production as quickly as possible, and it was vital to export everything they could make in order to bring currency into the country to pay off war debts. Part of Lyons's early strategy was to set the scene for the future of the business. Firstly the Swallow Sidecar Company was sold off, clearing the decks for full-scale car production, and secondly Jaguar Cars Limited was formed, confirming the end of the SS name due to its obvious Nazi connotations.

Early post-war production centred round modified versions of the pre-war saloons for obvious reasons. With little time to develop an entirely new model, and with strong demand for any cars available plus the need to export, Jaguar, like all other British manufacturers, had to make do with what they had.

Then, with entirely new models leading the company into the 1950s came well-produced, large format brochures, although apart from the principal launch brochures for some cars subsequent examples lacked much of the panache of earlier copy. As its models developed through the decade it is clear that Jaguar had so much success in selling their cars around the world that the same emphasis on promotional material was not necessary. This could have been attributable to cost cutting as well, so brochures became less extravagant and exciting except at the launch of an entirely new model.

Throughout this period Jaguar concentrated mainly on the use of stylised paintings and drawings to emphasise and positively enhance the look of its cars. In our politically correct times such material would not be allowed!

The Swinging Sixties

The 1960s was an expanding period for Jaguar, with an ever-increasing model range and company acquisitions such as the addition of the Daimler marque to its portfolio. The 1960s also heralded in a new approach to brochure production: out went stylised imagery in the main, and in came deliberately posed professional colour photography, and even studio work – in fact a new assertive approach to marketing and presentation.

A wide variety of material was produced during this period, including 'range' brochures and, surprisingly, even some black-and-white printed material to keep costs down.

The 1970s and the British Leyland era

Despite the launch of one of Jaguar's most significant models, the XJ6, and the fact that some brochures still reflected high quality and prestige, it was inevitable that the corporate influence of BL would have its effects. Eventually this led to the sharing of resources such as photographers, design, and production, and then to combined brochures aligning Jaguar with such cars as the Austin Allegro and Morris Marina, none of which did any good for Jaguar's street-cred.

The 1980s and beyond – a new confidence

The next decade saw a steady improvement during the final years of BL involvement in Jaguar's affairs. There was a new man at the helm (John Egan), a new slogan ('The Legend Grows'), and a more professional and confident approach to brochures and marketing in general. That confidence expanded into the 1990s with a larger range of cars and the need to satisfy a wider audience with marketing material in order to meet the demands of an increasingly competitive market.

In the following chapters we will explore the rich diversity of material produced by and for SS and Jaguar over three-quarters of a century.

The early days

1931 to 1948

We start our analysis after the company's move to Coventry and the announcement of the SS models. Lyons was by nature a salesman and initially became the main marketing force in the company. With the move to Foleshill in Coventry in 1928 it was he who decided that they should expand into the design and production of their own cars under the marque name of SS.

The **Motor**, *March 21, 1933.*

A SWALLOW PRODUCTION

MAGNIFICENCE THAT IS ONLY EXCELLED BY SS PERFORMANCE

" It is relatively easy to produce a low Sports Car
" of striking appearance, but it is not so simple a
" matter to produce such a Model with what
" might be termed sensible seating accommodation.
" These two features have been combined in both
" the S.S.1 and S.S.2 Cars. . . . From the driver's
" seat the long bonnet line of either Model is very
" impressive and suggestive of speed—a fact which
" is not belied by the performance of the Cars on
" the road. . . . IT IS REALLY ON THE OPEN
" ROAD, HOWEVER, THAT THESE S.S. MODELS
" COME INTO THEIR OWN. . . ."
—" The Motor," Jan. 31st.

Of 63 British Cars of all types, sizes and prices
tested a short while ago by the " The Autocar"
there was **not one Saloon Model of any des-**
cription which equalled the amazing performance
of the S.S.1 in the three essential features—
maximum speed, acceleration, and braking test.
The Car nearest in all-round performance to the
S.S.1 was priced at £875 !

The S.S.I (16 h.p.) is **£325**

The S.S.II (9 h.p.) is **£210**

HENLYS
S.S. DISTRIBUTORS for SOUTHERN ENGLAND
DEVONSHIRE HOUSE
PICCADILLY, W.1

HENLY HOUSE, EUSTON RD.
LONDON, N.W.1
Museum 7734
and at Bournemouth and Manchester

Swallow Coachbuilding Co., Ltd.
FOLESHILL, COVENTRY
(Coventry 8027)
MANUFACTURERS

The name and address of the S.S. agent
in your district will be sent immediately
on request

A HENLY IDEA !

LEFT *Impressive full-page colour advertisement from The Motor magazine in 1933, penned by the Nelson organisation. By this time the SS logo has taken prominence (appearing three times in the same advertisement), with Henlys and Swallow much reduced. Reproduced from The Motor, 21 March 1933.*

The new cars were introduced in 1931. The SS1 Coupé was based on the Standard Motor Company's Sixteen chassis, and the SS2 Coupé, a smaller model, was based on Standard's Little Nine. The Lyons philosophy of style and presence certainly came through in these early cars with rakish styling, low slung bodywork, elongated bonnet, and luxurious interior. As one journalist at the time quipped 'the £1,000 look for just £310', which was all the SS1 cost.

SS was an unknown make at the time and Lyons had to work hard to establish the 'product'. Off to a good start in offering superb value for money, the Lyons keenness for marketing also showed through in the paper material produced to 'sell' the new cars, in which he focused on the aspirational aspects of owning them.

Typical of the Lyons razzmatazz of the time were the magazine advertisements leading up to the introduction of the SS. Despite their emphasis on the Swallow-bodied cars, the strapline proclaimed 'WAIT! The SS is coming'.

The new cars were publicly announced in January 1932 and by September SS had purchased the front cover of the popular *Autocar* weekly magazine to promote them. SS became quite prolific at promotion through the car magazines, frequently taking the front cover. In those days front covers were the domain of a publisher's advertising department, and were a highly lucrative asset paid for by the advertiser. In return it gave the advertiser maximum coverage and instant recognition, an excellent ploy when trying to establish a new marque or promote a specific model.

Not all early SS advertising was paid for by the company. It didn't take long to appoint 18 distributors in the UK – amongst them the Henlys group, which had supported Lyons since the early days – so local advertising and even some national promotion would be handled by them. By 1930 one of the key people from Henlys had started his own advertising agency, Nelson Advertising, which got work from Henlys and, of course, Swallow/SS. Thus started

BELOW *This early fold-out leaflet for the SS1 followed the same style as Swallow material. This example depicts a stylised version of the car based on Lyons's original concept. The 'production' model looked quite different!*

FAR RIGHT TOP *This 1935 folder on the SS range is much simpler with less emphasis on information and a strange mix of stylised (almost toy-like) images alongside the well-executed drawing of the Airline model.*

FAR RIGHT BELOW *Similar imagery and text but more extensive information in the brochure, including 'Recent Achievements' in competition.*

a long association between Lyons and Nelson that influenced much of the promotional material produced for the cars. It was they who came up with many of the company's early slogans, such as 'The Value of its Beauty...The Beauty of its Value'. They also came up with the 'Jaguar' name and later borrowed and modified a motto used by MG in the 1930s – 'For Space...For Grace...For Pace'.

Lyons was an avid supporter of the Art Deco movement, very popular in the 1920s and early 1930s, these days epitomised by such popular TV programmes as *Poirot*. It is therefore no surprise that material produced for the SS range would take this theme.

Normal practice then, and for many years thereafter, was for promotional material to follow one of three routes: lavish multi-page brochures, nicely bound, printed on good

quality paper, sometimes with additional touches such as stick-ons, tassels, or ribbons, primarily intended for serious buyers; folders produced on cheaper paper, usually single large-scale sheets folded to create a multi-page document depicting single or multiple models, much cheaper to produce and ideal for motor show purposes; and range material, similar to the folders but carrying brief information and pictures of a whole range of vehicles produced by the manufacturer.

In its early days SS concentrated on the prestigious brochures and the range folders. Emphasising the need to market new cars and the expansion of model ranges, full-blown brochures and folders were produced each and every year from 1931, despite the obvious cost involved. For 1933 revised models were being announced with longer bodies, flowing wings,

RIGHT *Comparative material for 1933/34: the standard issue folder and lavish brochure equivalent with cord tie, relief lining, and the green and gold embossed logo.*

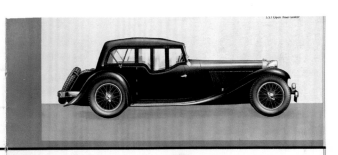

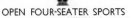

THE 2½ LITRE JAGUAR "100"

£305

and improved performance, and new versions such as the Tourer, Four Light saloon and, eventually, the Airline and Drop Head Coupé were added.

The quality brochures of the 1930s covering the SS range were lavish even by the standards of the day. Bound with stiff covers and making excellent use of pictures inside – although still only using two-colour printing to keep costs down – each model was depicted, with detailed description and specification. The still relatively new SS logo appeared prominently on the front cover and on every page.

The importance of marketing and public awareness is emphasised by the company's decision in 1934 to employ a specialist in this field. This was Ernest Rankin, who had also created the Red Barrel emblem for Watneys Brewery. He stayed with the company until his retirement in the 1960s.

Looking at the 1934 SS Cars prestige brochure as an example of Rankin's work, it typifies the quality approach that Lyons approved of for his cars. An expensive affair, it has 24 pages and stiff parchment covers, and the

SS logo and emblem feature prominently. Although still printed in just two colours it is extensively illustrated and features images and information on competitive achievements in motor sport. There is even a reproduction of the specially commissioned Gordon Crosby painting of the 1934 Alpine Rally featuring an SS1 Tourer. A lovely evocative way to market your cars! Interestingly, a green border and background is used throughout this brochure, a colour with which Jaguar has been associated for years.

Early entry into the world of Jaguar

In 1934 SS Cars Limited was formed as a separate company responsible for car production, which led, in 1935, to the launch of the name Jaguar, then merely a model name for an entirely new SS model. This new SS Jaguar saloon, launched in September 1935 at the Mayfair Hotel in London, offered luxury, superb styling, and excellent performance from its heavily modified, overhead valve version of the

ABOVE LEFT From 1935 the winged emblem took prominence, beautifully featured on the front cover of this brochure in metal-foil relief. Note the Jaguar name also coming to the fore.

ABOVE RIGHT One of the splendidly drawn images from the 1937 version of the 1935 'winged' brochure, of the SS100 against a Brooklands background.

An interesting new marketing concept was adopted by SS with the launch of the Jaguar saloon – a six-page leaflet showing all the models (including the original SS1 and 2).

This was printed and distributed with the contemporary Autocar and Motor magazines, an approach still followed by many manufacturers today.

Standard six-cylinder engine, all for the incredibly low price of just £385.

At the time of the SS Jaguar launch, out of the 367,000 British cars produced, 88 per cent were from large manufacturers such as Rootes, Ford, Morris, and Standard, leaving a relatively small market for the more prestigious brands, so competition was fierce. With this in mind, and disregarding the cheaper folders and introductory material, SS needed to hit the road running in order to capture some of this market. Its luxury brochures for the late 1930s were therefore larger than before, and just as – or more – prestigious than those of other manufacturers.

In 1937, for example, although the internal content was very similar to the 'winged' brochure pictured before, a new stylised jaguar head appeared, pre-empting the move to the modern 'leaper' motif. Also predating some of the better-known Jaguar mottos, this brochure used the French 'Celeriter et Silentio' phrase, which translated meant 'Swift and Silent'. Just as surprising, out went the SS logo in favour of just the word 'Jaguar' – as if to confirm early thoughts of abandoning the SS name entirely, something we know Lyons had considered pre-war but never carried through.

This brings us to 1938, with SS finely honing their brochure design to a new level, clearly embodying the style and flair of Lyons and his cars. This has to be considered one of the finest brochures the company ever produced. It was

LEFT *This most luxurious of SS brochures for 1938 featured all the latest model updates, including the new 3½-litre saloon. The quality of reproduction is exemplary. It is displayed here with the equivalent post-war miniature version (see later text).*

LEFT *An example of the superb later artwork for the SS Jaguar models taken from the 1938 brochure, in this case of the 3½-litre saloon. Other images included detailed drawings, colour schemes, optional extras, and once again 'Recent Competition Successes'.*

23

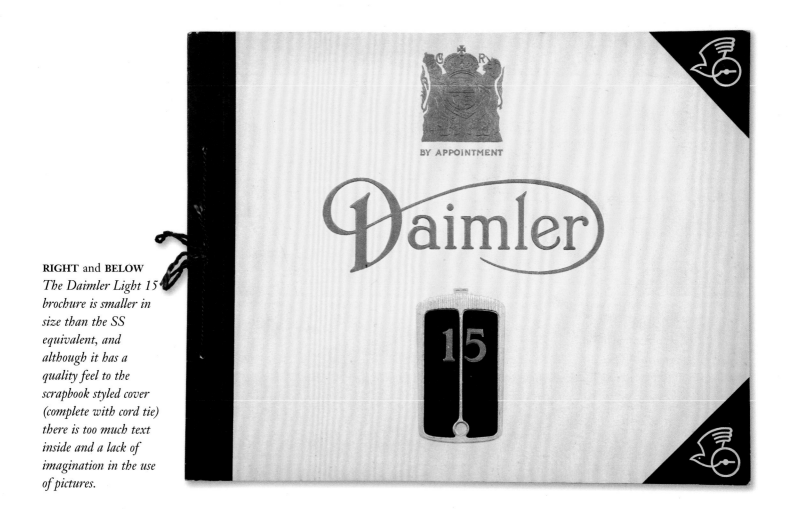

RIGHT and **BELOW**
*The Daimler Light 15
brochure is smaller in
size than the SS
equivalent, and
although it has a
quality feel to the
scrapbook styled cover
(complete with cord tie)
there is too much text
inside and a lack of
imagination in the use
of pictures.*

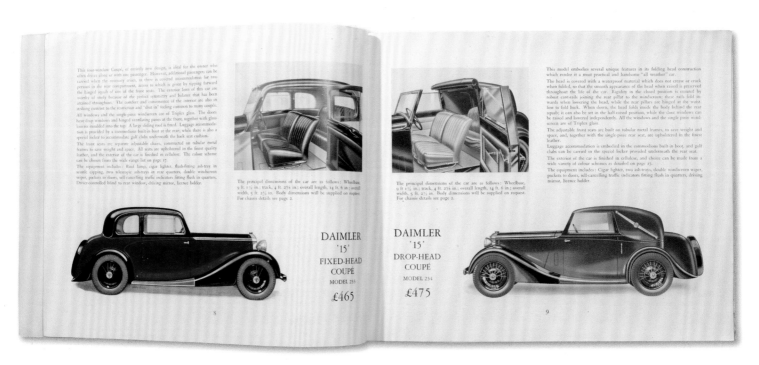

DAIMLER
'15'
FIXED-HEAD
COUPÉ
MODEL 255

£465

DAIMLER
'15'
DROP-HEAD
COUPÉ
MODEL 254

£475

another new look, with a simple, contemporary black cover simply stating the name Jaguar, the first use of this font with the dropped 'J'. This brochure oozed quality, with onion-skin frontispiece, new text, and entirely new full colour paintings of each model in double page spreads, accompanied by their specifications.

For 1939 and 1940 this brochure was reprinted with gold hot-foil lettering on the cover and page tabs to indicate model updates. Not only did this save money, but it also, perhaps, further emphasised the brochure's excellence.

Contemporary comparisons

Such was the quality of the pre-war SS material that it is worth comparing it to that of other manufacturers of the period. The pictures here give a good indication of how advanced the SS

material was, particularly when compared to more prestigious makers and those who produced far more vehicles.

At this point it is also worth reflecting on magazine advertising development during the early years of the marque. SS was really the only small-scale manufacturer to take advantage of the front covers of motor magazines, and depicted on page 27 are examples of how that treatment changed during this interim period.

Post-war revival

After the war, with the sale of the sidecar business and the change of name from SS to Jaguar, the production of vehicles followed pre-war practice except for minor trim and mechanical changes, the adoption of the Jaguar name on the cars, and the demise of the low production SS100 sports car.

BELOW *A complete contrast is this 1930s Rolls-Royce brochure with 54 pages, spiral-bound but very poorly produced. Even the tipped-in photographs are hand-colour finished and don't show the cars to best effect. Very Victorian compared to the modern approach of SS.*

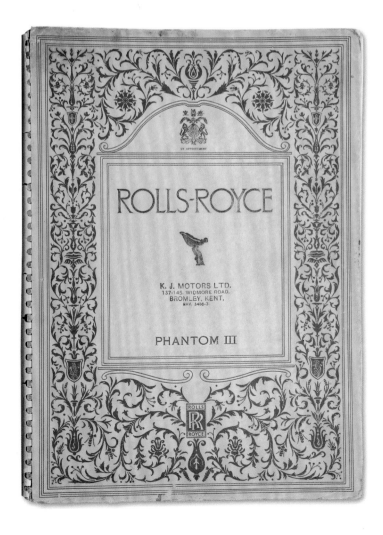

With major restrictions on new car sales in the UK, and the need to export to bring funds back into the country to pay off war debts, emphasis had to be given to overseas markets. Restrictions were in place over the use of raw and finished materials, not least paper, so to get round this Ernest Rankin instigated the printing of an approximately quarter-scale version of the prestigious pre-war brochure – an imaginative approach that ensured marketing material was available in the immediate post-war period. Measuring just 3¾in x 2¾in (95mm x 70mm), it wasn't just a simple reduction of the pre-war material, as some of the text had to be altered and deleted in order for it to remain legible.

It is worth reproducing in full Jaguar's explanation for its size as printed in this minute brochure: 'Severe restrictions on the use of paper have rendered it impossible for us to produce a full-sized catalogue in sufficient numbers to meet public demand for details of the new Jaguar. Therefore this miniature catalogue has been produced in order to give the greatest amount of information to the largest possible number of people, and in this tiny volume will be found all the particulars normally presented in a catalogue ten times its size.'

Interim model – the Mark V

However anyone cares to look at it, Jaguar's Mark V was merely an interim model designed to boost sales and to act as a test-bed for the entirely new chassis destined for a major new car launch in 1950. Introduced in 1948 both as a saloon and Drop Head Coupé, it was the only volume car produced by Jaguar until the introduction of the Mark VII two years later. Despite being substantially based on pre-war styling cues from the older models, the Mark V was undoubtedly more contemporary, dripping in chrome and with an enhanced interior. Although it still used the old Standard-derived pushrod engines (now built in-house at Jaguar), it had a new suspension and chassis layout that made it a very agile sporting saloon.

Although it is covered in the next chapter, mention must also be made here of the other new Jaguar launched in 1948, the XK120 sports car, since the mammoth prestige launch brochure for the Mark V also incorporated the sports car. Interesting, for historical reasons, is the fact that both the six-cylinder (XK120) and the stillborn four-cylinder (XK100) were featured.

The Mark V brochure represents another landmark in Jaguar published material. Of very large format, spiral bound, with a stiff mottled

The 25 h.p. Limousine ... and an impression of the Landaulette

LEFT *January 1937: Reflecting the luxury brochure of the period, the use of the jaguar animal comes to the fore as if to emphasise the name 'Jaguar'. In fact the SS insignia is already starting to take a back seat.*

BELOW *October 1937: Only nine months later, for the British Motor Show issue, the company's advertising shows much more confidence, as the car is now established. The use of a shadowy image is enough, plus the SS insignia has been removed entirely. Also note the motto: 'Swift as the Wind – Silent as a Shadow'!*

BOTTOM LEFT *March 1939: The cars are doing exceptionally well, and such confidence inspires the prominence of just the name and emblem now. Jaguar is established.*

TOP RIGHT *July 1939: A special feature in this Motor magazine prompted Jaguar and its dealers to take a significant amount of advertising space. Here the double-page company spread promoting the 1940 models doesn't mention SS anywhere.*

RIGHT *The same July 1939 magazine: a dealer advertising promotion, but the page headings clearly show that the emphasis is on Jaguar, not SS.*

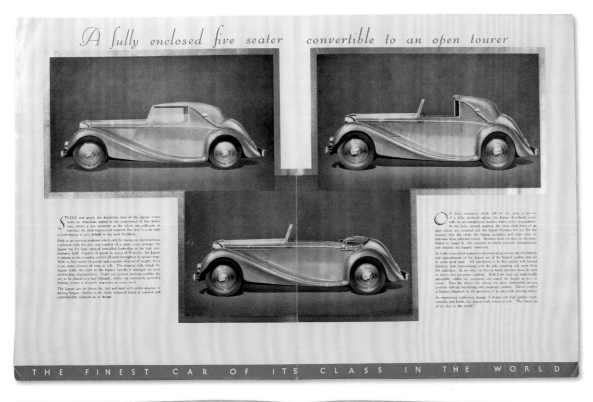

A fully enclosed five seater convertible to an open tourer

THE FINEST CAR OF ITS CLASS IN THE WORLD

THE AUTOCAR, October 1, 1948

The new drophead coupé on 2½ and 3½ litre chassis

The Jaguar Drop Head Coupé with its elegant flowing lines has an irresistible appeal for the motorist who, whilst desiring a body with touring-car characteristics yet requires, on occasion, the snug protection of a fully-enclosed saloon. It has all the new features and many improvements of the saloon illustrated overleaf including independent front suspension, new frame, new hydraulic brakes, new transmission system and fifteen other important improvements. As with the saloon, no startling departure has been made from the dignity and good taste which critics the world over have declared to be inherent characteristics of Jaguar design. The new Jaguar is better, finer looking but still unmistakably a Jaguar, and more than ever the finest car of its class in the world.

19 important new features

(1) Independent Front Suspension. (2) Fully hydraulic Two-leading shoe Girling Brakes. (3) Entirely new frame. (4) New Burman-Douglas re-circulating ball-type steering. (5) New transmission system. (6) Longer rear springs with new P.V.7 Girling Dampers. (7) Pressed steel wide rim base wheels, fitted with Dunlop 6.70 x 16 Super Comfort Tyres. (8) Increased interior dimensions. (9) Flat floor. (10) New luxurious unpleated upholstery. (11) Increased all-round visibility. (12) Increased leg room. (13) Built-in headlamps. (14) New instrument panel, illuminated by infra-red ray. (15) Twin bumpers with over-riders. (16) Concealed door hinges. (17) Press button door handles. (18) New and improved air-conditioning system. (19) Dust-free zip fastener door pockets.

Jaguar THE FINEST CAR OF ITS CLASS IN THE WORLD

TOP LEFT *Despite restrictions and cost in relation to the small-scale production of the Drop Head Coupé models, a separate, unique four-page folder was published for these models. It might be conjectured that this was primarily produced with the overseas market in mind.*

LEFT *Pre-launch, simple folders were produced for the Mark V, one specifically for the saloon, the other for the Drop Head Coupé. With stylised drawings and headed 'The Realisation of an Ideal', they heralded in the new model. This six-page folder was also issued using the UK weekly car magazines for distribution.*

Jaguar

THE FINEST CAR OF ITS CLASS IN THE WORLD

JAGUAR CARS LIMITED, COVENTRY (Previously S.S. Cars Ltd.)

2½ LITRE *Specification* SALOON

● *Traduction Française page 23* ● *Deutsche Uebersetzung Seite 23* ● *Traducción Española pagina 23*

ENGINE. Six cylinder Jaguar Mark 2J litre ; 73 mm. bore ; 106 mm. stroke ; 2,663·7 c.c. developing 102 b.h.p. at 4,600 r.p.m. ; overhead large diameter valves, push rod operated ; 2½ ins. diameter counterweighted crankshaft carried in seven large precision made steel backed bearings ; connecting rods of light alloy ; chrome-iron cylinder block ; detachable head ; compression ratio 7·3 ; cooling by pump circulation with by-pass thermostat control ; submerged oil pump ; forced lubrication throughout, complete circulation through full flow oil filter ; special Lucas de luxe coil and distributor ignition system ; twin S.U. carburetters with electrically controlled automatic choke.

FRAME. Straight plane steel box section frame of immense strength and stiffness. Torsional rigidity is ensured by 7 ins. deep channel cross bracings and massive box section front cross member.

TRANSMISSION. Four-speed synchromesh gearbox of improved design. Single helical gears with strengthened teeth mounted in needle roller bearings. Gear ratios : 1st 15·35 ; 2nd 9·01 ; 3rd 6·21 ; top 4·55. Hardy Spicer all metal divided propeller shaft. Borg & Beck 9 ins. diameter single dry plate clutch. Centrally-placed gear lever with remote control.

SUSPENSION. Independent front suspension incorporating wishbone and torsion bar principle. Direct acting hydraulic shock absorbers. Rear suspension by long slow-movement steel leaf springs with blades tapered and tapered to give flexibility and silence in operation, controlled by piston type dampers. Rear springs totally enclosed in gaiters fitted with grease nipples.

BRAKES. Full hydraulic two-leading-shoe brakes with 12 ins. diameter high duty iron drums 2½ ins. wide. Friction lining area, 164 square inches. Front drums fitted with cooling ducts. Pistol grip handbrake on rear wheels only through separate linkage.

STEERING. Burman re-circulating ball type steering, positive and accurate at all speeds. Bluemel 18" adjustable steering wheel. Left or right hand steering optional.

WHEELS AND TYRES. Heavily dished pressed steel bolt on type with wide base rims carry Dunlop super comfort 6·70 ins. × 16 ins. tyres.

FUEL SUPPLY. By electric pump from 14 gallon rear tank with reserve supply and warning light. Petrol filler cap concealed in rear wing and fitted with lock.

ELECTRIC EQUIPMENT. Lucas de luxe 12 volt set with ventilated dynamo ; 64 amp. capacity battery ; 10 hour discharge ; built-in head lamps and wing lamps ; two fog lamps ; stop lights ; reverse light ; twin rear lights ; two interior lights with extra door-controlled interior illumination ; twin blended note horns ; twin-bladed screen wiper ; cigar lighter.

INSTRUMENTS. 5 ins. diameter 120 m.p.h. speedometer, with headlamp beam warning light, 5 ins. diameter rev-olution counter, ammeter, oil pressure gauge, water temperature gauge, petrol gauge, clock, self-cancelling trafficators with warning light.

AIR CONDITIONING. Built-in air conditioning unit incorporating de-froster and de-mister. Improved system of induction provides cold filtered air taken from outside car for ventilating the interior during hot weather and fresh warm air for cold conditions.

UPHOLSTERY AND CARPETING. Upholstered throughout in finest quality Vaumol leather hide and Dunloppillo. Flat floor is thickly carpeted over felt underlay.

SEATING. Front bucket seats adjustable for height and reach. Heavily padded folding central arm-rest in rear compartment.

INTERIOR APPOINTMENTS. Garnish rails, window frames and instrument panels are of fine quality wood in polished figured walnut finish, press button door handles, capacious soft leather door pockets with zip fasteners, large cubby lockers, ventilator windows in front and rear compartments, glove drawer, ash trays.

SPARE WHEELS AND TOOLS. Spare wheel is carried in special compartment beneath luggage locker. Tools are housed individually in specially shaped weatherproof container in rear locker lid fitted with automatic catch.

LUGGAGE ACCOMMODATION. Ample accommodation is provided in the large rear locker, the lid of which may be lowered to form platform for additional luggage. Platform and locker interior highly polished and fitted with raised rubber protector strips.

EASY JACKING. Any wheel may be raised clear of the ground with the minimum of effort by means of special easy-lift jack.

PRINCIPAL DIMENSIONS. Wheel base, 10 ft. 0 ins. ; track front, 4 ft. 8 ins. ; rear, 4 ft. 9½ ins. ; overall length, 15 ft. 7½ ins ; overall width, 5 ft. 9½ ins. ; overall height, 5 ft. 2½ ins. ; unladen turning circle, 35 ft. 0 ins. ; dry weight, 33 cwts. (approx.).

KEY TO SEATING DIAGRAMS

	MAX.		MIN.	
	Ins.	Cm.	Ins.	Cm.
A	16½	41-64	10½	26-40
B	4·2	106-68	33	83-82
C	14½	36-86	12½	31-48
D	4	10-16	2	5-08
E	26	91-44	34	86-36
F	18	45-72	9	22-86

The capacious luggage compartment is fitted with rubber protector strips, the lid forming a platform for additional luggage. Tools are carried in the lid (see page 8).

Instrument panels of all closed models are of seasoned wood with polished figured walnut finish. The glass drawer at the bottom centre can be retained to accommodate wireless control panel.

Page 7

THE MARK V JAGUAR 2½ LITRE SALOON

Page 6

FAR LEFT *'The finest car of its class in the world' – confidence indeed on this post-war advertising poster.*

LEFT and **BELOW** *Jaguar had some of the best artists around to produce images like this for the Mark V brochure and other uses.*

BELOW *Despite the originally intended low production status of the new XK sports car, it got incredible coverage in the 1948 brochure, which also included a full specification for the XK100 model that was never produced. Alongside is the not-so-prestigious price list for all the models; not surprisingly, the four-cylinder XK didn't sell at the same price as the larger-engined version!*

beige cover with the Jaguar name and the winged logo embossed into a large foil square, glued in and bordered, it shouts 'quality'. The superbly painted, coloured images of each model are produced on high quality paper tipped onto textured board, each car getting a full double-page spread with accompanying specifications and inset detail pictures. The main body of text was printed in English, French, German and Italian (with colour coding), and at the back there was even a full-page hand-coloured aerial view of the factory in Foleshill.

In its own way this brochure introduced what the author considers 'artistic licence', in that the artists tended to depict the cars at their best, even if, at times, this was actually better than the real thing! Examples are the dashboard veneer

and the extensive rear compartment legroom, the picture of the rear interior compartment clearly depicting enormous legroom without the front seats being present.

This brochure was of such high quality that in the words of the US importer at the time 'the cars sold on the basis of the brochure alone'.

Other, cheaper sales material in the form of folders was also available for the Mark V, and Jaguar continued to feature the car prominently in magazines, in full colour on the front covers of many, alongside the XK sports car.

Jaguar's model range was due to take a major leap forward in the 1950s with mass production methods being adopted for the XK and the launch of the big Mark VII saloon, as well as for smaller-bodied models.

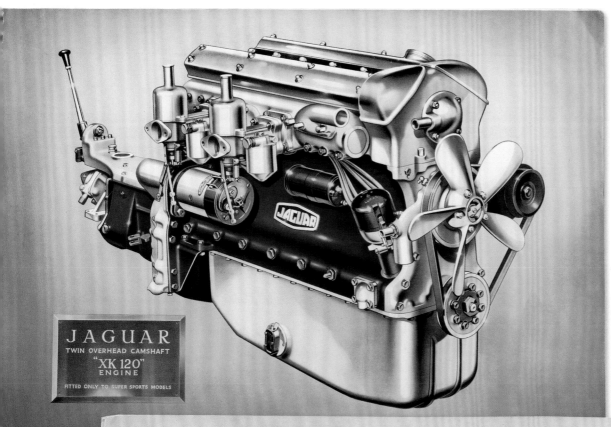

JAGUAR
TWIN OVERHEAD CAMSHAFT
"XK 120"
ENGINE
FITTED ONLY TO SUPER SPORTS MODELS

LEFT and **BELOW**
The drawings of the black XK120 roadster are taken from an early car and clearly show subtle differences to mainstream production models. Note, for example, the one-piece rear bumper attached to the boot lid, a feature that never appeared. The significance of the XK power unit is testified by its appearance on the opposite page, although on the next page the old pushrod engine still received significant coverage.

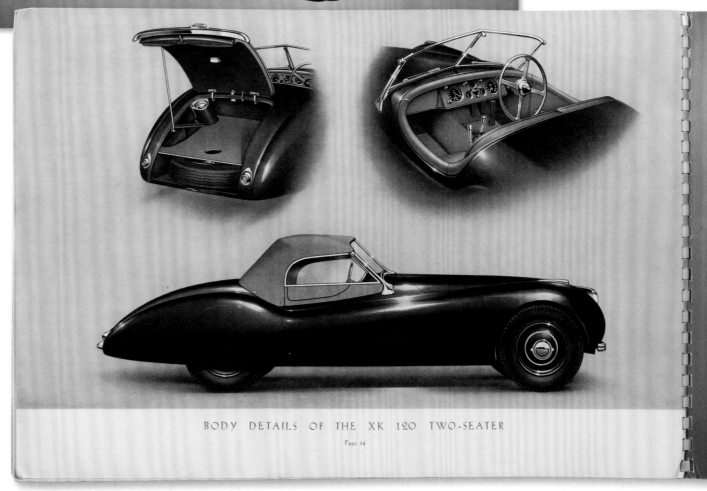

BODY DETAILS OF THE XK 120 TWO-SEATER

Page 14

JAGUAR

JAGUAR CARS LTD.
COVENTRY

XK 140 MODELS

THE XK150 JAGUAR

A new luxur...

Here to join the world-famous Mark V...
litre models is the Mark Eight—one of the...
models ever offered as a series production...
furnishings, cabinet work, fitments and acce...
the tradition of refinement and craftsman...
associated only with the art of specialist co...
whilst a degree of mechanical refinement has bee...
which stamps this car as outstanding even am...
distinguished Jaguar range which it now joins...
preserving the basic lines of the Mark VII, the Ma...
has its own distinctive frontal appearance and is off...
a wide range of two-tone exterior colours. It is a...

Successes
Dunlop Disc Brakes —

1952 **First** : Rheims Sports Car Race.
First : Silverstone Production Sports Car Race.

1953 **First, Second, Fourth** : Le Mans 24-hour Race
First : Rheims 12-hour Race

1954 **Second, Fourth** : Le Mans 24-hour Race
First, Second, Third : Rheims 12-hour Race

1955 **First** : Sebring 12-hour Race
First, Third : Le Mans 24 hour Race

1956 **First, Fourth, Sixth** : Le Mans 24-hour Race
First, Second, Third, Fourth : Rheims Sports Car Race

expert opinion...

JAGUAR
XK 150

XK 140 open 2-seater

XK 140 Hard Top Coupe

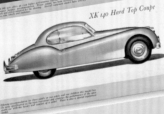

Part...
in...

NEW XK150 DISC BR

JAGUAR
range of models for 1955

The 1950s – *'Grace, Space and Pace'*

As it entered the 1950s the British motor industry was breaking free from the effects of the Second World War. The Jaguar brand was now well established, the Mark V had revitalised saloon sales, and the XK120 had proved so embarrassingly popular that the company had to move to volume production with a steel bodyshell to meet demand.

In the last chapter we covered the marketing debut of the XK sports car in 1948 as an integral part of the splendid Mark V brochure. This indeed echoes the well-known fact that, at the time, the sports car was merely meant to tantalise and create interest in what Jaguar conceived as a far more important new car to come, the Mark VII. As it turned out this is one of the rare occasions when William Lyons got it wrong and underestimated the enthusiasm and demand for the new sports car.

During that first 12 months of XK120 availability (virtually in hand-built form) even Jaguar didn't know the right direction to take, as much of the early media information couldn't even determine the right name for the car – 'XK120 Super Sports', '3½-litre Super Sports', '2 Seater type XK120', 'XK Super Sports 2 Seater', or just 'Super Sports'.

In preparing for volume production attention also had to be given to promotional material, remembering that by 1950 the Mark V was going out of production so that the joint-car material would be superfluous. The first XK-specific brochure was released the same year, early print-runs still retaining details of the XK100. Although large in size, it was only eight pages, used copy and images from the previous material, and was not a particularly luxurious offering. It is therefore an excellent example of the emphasis the company put on its saloon car models, always destined to be produced in much larger numbers than its sports cars and, indeed, to be the major profit earners for Jaguar.

This brochure was reprinted and amended a couple of times during the life of the XK120, adapting to model changes, and is the only brochure produced on the Roadster model.

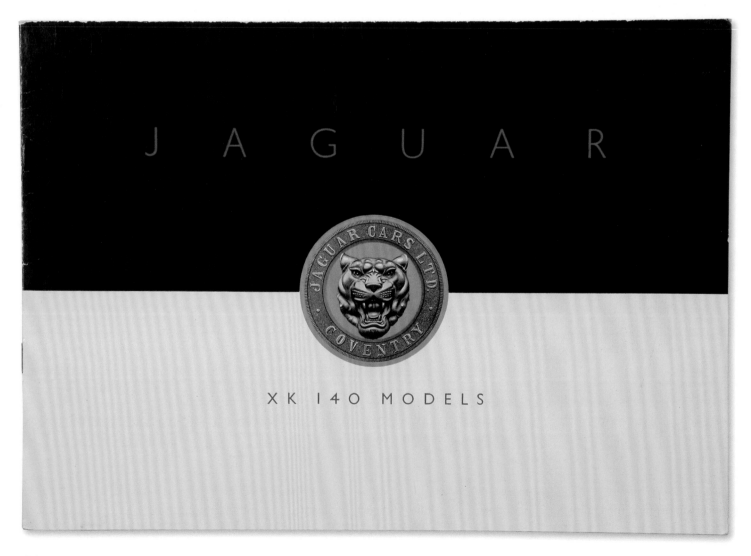

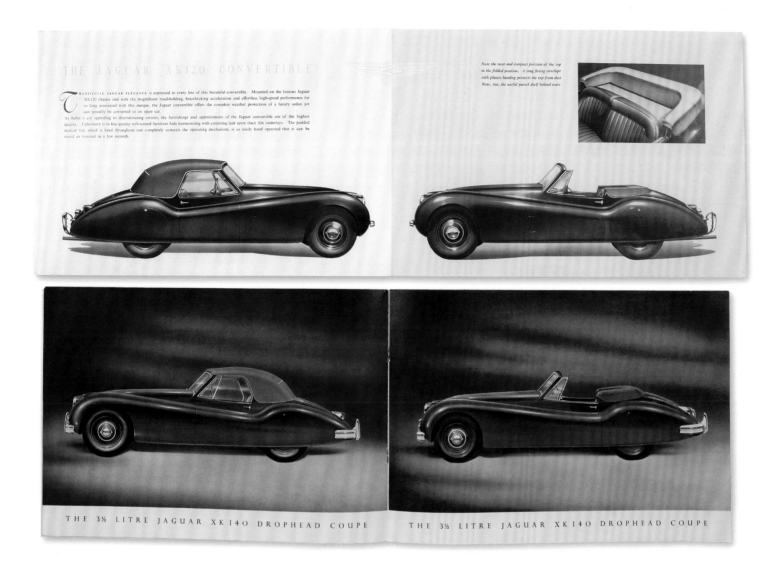

XK expansion

It became common practice for Jaguar to introduce ranges of models based on the same theme – an ideal way to expand the market, increase production and bring down unit costs that is still common today, used by all manner of manufacturers. Alongside the all-steel Roadster a brilliant new Fixed Head Coupé version was announced. The beauty of this car was that it offered real grand tourer motoring in saloon car comfort but with the handling capabilities and performance of the sports car. Such features as the wind-up windows and exterior door handles were still virtually unheard of in a sports car. Surprisingly, near the end of XK120 production Jaguar released another new variant, the Drop

Head Coupé, incorporating features from the Fixed Head Coupé and the Roadster, to create a very stylish and practical convertible model.

Jaguar created special folders for each of these variants, which cut the cost of producing an entirely new marketing tool for all the XKs. The fact that these were simple four-page items in two-colour printing re-emphasised the importance of the high volume saloons.

Jaguar again took the initiative with regular front cover coverage for the XK120 in the car magazines.

XK140 to 150

The XK sports car featured throughout the 1950s, the next development coming in 1954 with the new XK140. Changes were significant enough to dictate a new brochure, plus the by now obligatory and cheaper folder as well.

In contrast to the confusion over the launch of the XK120 and the complications of later additional models, the XK140 was much easier to cover. An obvious and logical development from the earlier models, its launch (in all three body styles) and marketplace was well understood and carefully planned for. Several versions of a simple four-page folder were produced, but more importantly so was a high quality, but smaller at only 11in x 8in (279mm x 203mm), brochure.

Within the brochure's 12 pages, typically well-produced colour artwork featured in the usual double-page spread format with other information. There are some interesting aspects to this brochure; for example, the first picture of a bronze XK140 Roadster is clearly just a re-touched and coloured version of that used for

the XK120 earlier. Similarly, the centre-page layout of the two Drop Head Coupé models (with hoods up and down) is another retouched version of the XK120.

Two versions of this prestige brochure were produced, the second with a colour schemes listing at the back. It is somewhat of a surprise that such a fine quality brochure was produced for a model that only remained in production for three years and sold less than 10,000 examples. Another surprise is that despite Jaguar competition successes at this time, no mention at all is made of them in this material for a car appealing to sporting motorists – quite a contrast to the saloons (see below)!

Natural progression and new technology necessitated further upgrades to keep the model 'alive', and so the XK150 was announced in May 1957. This provides an interesting aspect of Jaguar publicity that has been followed many

LEFT and **BELOW**
The importance of the introduction of disc brakes prompted Dunlop (who developed and built the systems for Jaguar) to publish their own booklet on the subject with specific use of Jaguar images and quotations from their drivers, such as Mike Hawthorn.

RIGHT *A rather avant-garde approach was given to the cover of the XK150 Roadster brochure, the front of the XK leaping dramatically out from a circle of blue sky.*

BELOW *Examples of the incredible selection of magazine front covers designed to expose the Mark VII to the motoring public in the early 1950s.*

THE XK150 JAGUAR ROADSTER

THE 3½ LITRE JAGUAR MARK VII SALOON

times since, and was also applied to the large saloons from this period.

An entirely new car coming to launch deserves excellent publicity and brochure material – hence the hard work and finance put behind models like the Mark V; but as the models mature and need regular upgrading, less emphasis is given to publicity, particularly if (a) the cars are selling very well without it, or (b) money is being directed into an entirely new replacement project. Such was the case with the XK150, as the XK theme was now in the September of its years. There was still plenty of life left in the model, but the brochures, although adequate, were not of the highest standard.

Initially offered in only Fixed Head or Drop Head forms, the first rather plain white folder opened out into eight pages, poster style,

though not as before on paper stock but on stiff board to give it an air of quality. Printed with only black and white photographs, spot colour was used to highlight specific text and the growler logo on the front cover. The cover concentrated on the disc brake element of the new car, a major technological advance at the time.

This brochure was reprinted several times through 1958, 1959 and 1960 to take account of model changes, its quality deteriorating as time went on, but it never featured the Roadster model introduced in 1958.

A separate large-scale, four-page card folder was created for the Roadster model, something of a throwback to the early XK120 item. This was very uninspiring, its best feature being perhaps the front cover style and the use of silver ink.

ABOVE *This picture prepared for the launch brochure of the Mark VII is certainly not the best artwork used in Jaguar marketing material, particularly when compared to that used for the equivalent Bentley model from the early 1950s.*

BELOW *This poor quality artwork, cheaply produced for the later Mark VII models, also shows a lack of consistency in style. The black car is merely a poorly retouched picture from the earlier blue-tinted image shown on page 41, and the brown automatic transmission picture has an air of impressionist about it.*

The flagship saloons of the 1950s

The hard work put into the development of the six-cylinder Jaguar XK power unit had not been for the benefit of the sports car but, more importantly, for the next generation of Jaguar saloons, starting with the Mark VII introduced in 1950. Bringing together the then new chassis and suspension layout first seen in the interim Mark V and the XK engine released in the XK120, Jaguar introduced their new flagship saloon at the 1950 motor shows.

For many reasons a far more important new model than the Mark V it replaced, it was given significant coverage in contemporary motor magazines, not least as a regular feature on their front covers, yet the launch brochure material was a little disappointing.

Returning to the pre-war brochure size and with textured covers, the internal format was simpler with no colour imagery at all. Instead, a then common trait of using toned drawings was adopted, with a full-page image of a blue-tinted car within a spotlight beam. The artwork is quite poor by the standard of work like that produced for the Mark V, and the rest of the brochure content lacks inspiration, although there is a two-page spread of international XK engine competition successes accompanied by an interesting collage of black and white photographs of competing XK120s. This showed a move back to pre-war concepts again, and epitomises how competition was used to promote the sale of the volume saloons.

Though this was such an important new car for Jaguar, the marketing material lacked the

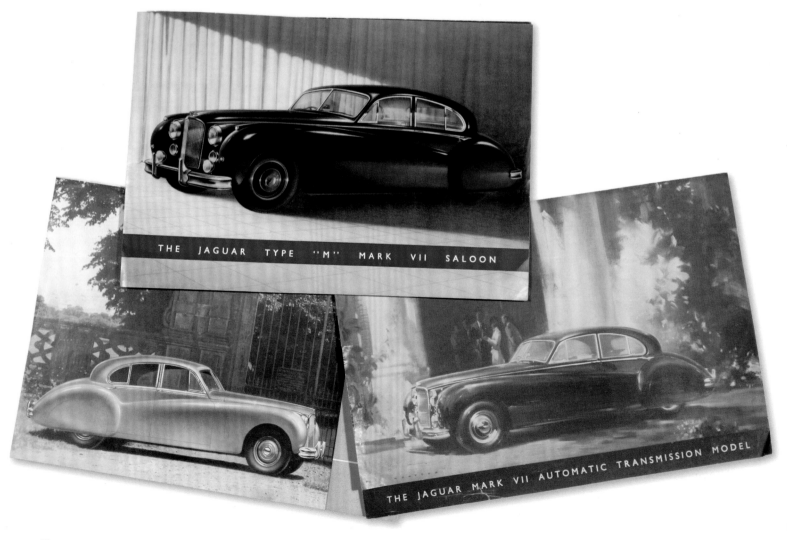

THE JAGUAR TYPE "M" MARK VII SALOON

THE JAGUAR MARK VII AUTOMATIC TRANSMISSION MODEL

A new luxury model now

Here to join the world-famous Mark VII, XK and 2.4 litre models is the Mark Eight—one of the most luxurious models ever offered as a series production car. Interior furnishings, cabinet work, fitments and accessories are in the tradition of refinement and craftsmanship usually associated only with the art of specialist coachbuilders, whilst a degree of mechanical refinement has been achieved which stamps this car as outstanding even amongst the distinguished Jaguar range which it now joins. Whilst preserving the basic lines of the Mark VII, the Mark Eight has its own distinctive frontal appearance and is offered in a wide range of two-tone exterior colours. It is available

sparkle of many of the company's pre-war offerings and the quality of post-war items from rivals producing less prestigious models, such as Riley and MG.

With the later addition of automatic transmission and overdrive models, Jaguar provided separate two-colour leaflets, although they didn't even follow the same theme. The automatic version opened upwards and had a bled-off cover picture of a drawn Mark VII against a somewhat impressionistic background. The overdrive leaflet had a more sombre cover with no image, opened from the right, and used a retouched picture of the car against a background of photographed gates. Even when the revised Mark VIIM was announced it only warranted a similar two-tone, single-fold leaflet.

Although the automatic transmission leaflet remained available, the overdrive version was short-lived as, later in 1954, Jaguar

announced their revised Mark VIIM model, which necessitated the publication of a new leaflet. Far less appealing than the original Mark VII material, it was an obvious move to reduce publicity costs for a model that was selling very nicely, thank you, without the need to advertise.

The Jaguar Mark VIII is interesting in that it was announced as an additional model to the Mark VIIM in 1957, offering a more powerful engine, more luxurious interior, and enhanced exterior style, yet it also continued to be listed as a model in its own right after the demise of the earlier car and the introduction of the Mark IX (cosmetically the same car as the Mark VIII but with disc brakes, power steering, and a larger engine).

The same dull treatment was given to the promotional material for these cars, although in both cases magazine advertising tended to be slightly more interesting.

ABOVE *Folders for the later flagship saloons: the Mark VIII benefited from superb artwork inside, while the Mark IX enjoyed the theme of speed and the open road.*

A new Jaguar masterpiece.....

that have gained for the name of Jaguar the highest international repute. For over a year Jaguar's engineers and technicians have worked to produce, not simply a new model, but an entirely new car of such outstanding merit as to be worthy of presentation to a world which has for long been accustomed to expect great things from Jaguar. How well they have succeeded is made manifest by the specification and performance of the 2·4 litre, a car which derives its character and breeding from every reward of

With all the inherent quality of its marque

The handsome instrument panel of the Special Equipment model.

The spacious and luxuriously appointed rear compartment permits of three passengers being carried with ease and in complete comfort. Seating is of finest Vaumol leather over Dunlopillo.

ABOVE *This careless rendition of the 2.4-litre Standard model (without mascot and fog lamps) couldn't have done much to promote sales of the car back in 1955.*

LEFT *Another example – like the early XK120 folder – of artists creating images for brochures taken from pre-production cars. In this case the dashboard bears little resemblance to production 2.4s and is taken from the car's launch material.*

Expansion into the compact saloon market

As the mid-1950s approached, Jaguar had experienced incredible success in sales and motoring competition and had received excellent media reports, but William Lyons had the foresight to realise that if the company was to continue to expand then it would need a larger range of cars. This led to the introduction of a new compact saloon.

Offering the same high standards as other Jaguar models, a new, stylish medium-sized saloon, offering performance at a reasonable price, would challenge a wider range of competitors. Suddenly the owners of cars like the Ford Zodiac, Vauxhall Cresta, Rover 90 and Humber Super Snipe were within Jaguar's sights. The resulting new model was to establish a line of similar cars that would span the next 14 years.

The 2.4 was launched at the British Motor Show in London in 1955, but, despite being the

company's most important model in terms of potential sales, the promotional literature was rather disappointing. The original item produced was no more than a folder that opened out poster style, with poor artwork that did not do the car justice. In fact it's amazing that William Lyons allowed it to be produced.

Given the poor image of the car that this material portrayed it is incredible that it was reprinted several times throughout the life of the 2.4.

In 1957 the range expanded to include the larger 3.4-litre model, which initially deserved a folder of its own. Of standard size, printed on board, this was in only two colours and had just four pages (single fold). Maybe the car was exciting, given its performance and the strapline on the cover, but inside the usual dull treatment

with another retouched black and white image couldn't have done much to promote it. But then, once again, it was selling on its own merit, without promotion!

With the introduction of disc brakes for these models and other rationalisation issues in production, the two models (2.4 and 3.4) came together for promotional purposes, firstly in the form of a rehashed, black and white version of the earlier 2.4 item, and then as a more striking new one, with a black and red cover, a return to colour inside, mention of disc brakes, and slightly improved paintings of the cars along with the correct dashboard.

All in all this was nevertheless a very poor offering in promotional material for such an important model, but this seems to be the case with most of the brochures produced by Jaguar during this period, none of which show the flair, ingenuity, and quality of pre-war offerings. In reality marketing was largely unnecessary at a time when the company could not produce enough cars to satisfy demand.

Overseas markets and range brochures

We have so far said little about the overseas literature produced to promote Jaguar models. This is because, in most cases, the same material was supplied for export markets unless the importers produced their own. Examples like the Mark V/XK brochure were printed in a selection of languages anyway.

In the mid-1950s, regular UK material was reprinted for some markets, particularly Germany, in their own language, the 3.4-litre Mark 1 brochure being a perfect example. Other countries tended to use the English language brochures. In the US, however, not only did they use UK material – in many cases overprinting the dealers' information and also

RIGHT *The poster-style spread of the last Mark 1 folder was slightly better.*

FAR RIGHT *XK140 material destined for the US market looks quite impressive from the cover with gold inking, but inside it lacks punch.*

The finest car of its class in the world

The Jaguar XK-140 is a direct descendant of the world-famous XK-120 and is now, more than ever, the yardstick by which the sports cars of the world are measured.

For luxurious appointments, comfort, brilliant performance, for sheer driving delight, the XK-140 is incomparable. It will be *the* car you'll be eager to drive be it a trip for groceries or a long jaunt over the highways.

Though the XK-140 engine is fierce and powerful when you want it so, the Jaguar's gentle tractability in traffic makes it a pleasure to drive under all conditions. Combine this with the car's superbly balanced suspension and light, precise rack and pinion steering . . . you'll find that driving becomes one of the greatest pleasures you've ever known.

The XK-140 is made in three body styles: the Sports Roadster (illustrated on the cover), the Convertible and the Hard Top Coupe. Overdrive is an optional extra on all three.

Modified cars are available at slight additional cost. This includes the "C" type cylinder head, raising the horse power from 190 to 220, special crankshaft damper, wire wheels, dual exhausts and fog lamps. Borg-Warner automatic transmission is available on the Coupe and Convertible.

The World-famous 3½ litre JAGUAR XK engine

This is the same phenomenal engine that has sped Jaguar cars to countless victories in major competition on European and U. S. circuits. Its double overhead camshaft design is the most modern in the world and is capable of powering the XK-140 to speeds near 140 m.p.h. with ease. Yet, its extreme flexibility makes it docile and smooth in stop and go city traffic. The XK engine is built for great reliability and long life.

★★★ Roadster — Divided seats individually adjustable for reach and upholstered in leather. The top is made of mohair material with unbreakable rear light—when folded, it is completely concealed behind seats. Detachable sidescreens stored in a tray in the hood compartment. Interior heater incorporating windshield defroster. Front end of trunk hinges down to increase storage for golf clubs, etc. Capacious pockets in doors.

★★★ Convertible — Two individually adjustable front seats with two seats behind, suitable for small children —all seats of British glove leather. Front end of trunk hinges down to increase storage for golf clubs, etc. Instrument panel and all interior trim finished in hand-rubbed walnut. Wind-up windows. Interior heater incorporating windshield defroster. The top is covered with mohair and has a fully lined interior which completely conceals the linkage.

Two individually adjustable front seats with seating accommodations in rear for one adult or two children—all seats of British glove leather. Front end of trunk hinges down to increase storage space for golf clubs, etc. Instrument panel and all interior trim finished in hand-rubbed walnut. Wind-up windows. Interior heater incorporating windshield defroster.

★★★ 2-3 seater Hard Top Coupe

Studron "A" Armory, N.Y.
Furs by Maximilian

LEFT TOP and
BOTTOM *Two other
examples of US-
produced material of the
1950s. The contrived
studio image of the 3.4
with polo riders doesn't
come off, and the
extensive use of dulling
spray on areas like the
bumper show a lack of
photographers' attention
to detail. They didn't
even bother to
straighten the 'Jaguar'
plate at the front of the
Mark IX – poor show
for what were very
expensive motor cars in
the States.*

*order. Soft tanned
*ubber. Side armrests
*ing armrest in rear
*abbed walnut cabinet
*os. Interior lighting.
*unrestricted – five

*lished walnut
*anel, garnish
*ou surrounds,
*ments, are in
ury tradition.

affixing prices in dollars – but they also printed unique material – mostly at the cost of the importer rather than Jaguar!

With the expansion of the company's models there was a renewed need for range brochures like those produced for Swallow and SS in the pre-war period, covering the full range of cars produced by Jaguar but in much less detail, a good source of material for motor shows and for those who just wanted to 'collect'.

Typical examples of US-produced model literature are depicted below and clearly show the lack of quality and attention to detail put into many of the UK equivalents.

The United States also produced several small range brochures, some not only small but also simple, consisting of monochrome literature on cheap paper. They offered little to the enthusiast and it is doubtful they did anything to further the Jaguar image in the US. All featured the same stylised front page ('Just for the fun of it!

ABOVE
Contemporary Jaguar North America full-page magazine advertisements for the 3.4 and Mark VIII.

The Distinguished British

297 W. COLORADO ST.,
PASADENA, CALIF.

JAGUAR

THE FINEST CAR IN ITS CLASS IN THE WORLD

3.4 SPORTS SEDAN—An entirely new experience on the road. Call it the ultimate luxury in a sports car, or sports car performance in a 4-door sedan. A family sedan with the unique features which have scored Jaguar wins in competitions the world over

XK 150
ROADSTER

This famous car now features one piece windshield, roll up windows, convertible top and four wheel disc brakes.

Available also as XK 150 "S", with "Straight port" Cylinder head, 3 HD8 S.U. carburetors, 9:1 compression ratio, 250 B.H.P.

XK
HARDTO

For the motorist car zest in a close famous XK eng same superb han the open model, vides comfort and s plus the thrill of petition perform Seats in rear fo children or one ad 4-wheel disc brake

the XK-SS two-seater super-sport
Available in limited quantities

Here, for the experienced sports car driver, is the translation of Jaguar experience in recent competition models into the broader category of the dual-purpose sports-racing machine. A high performance sports-touring car in the tradition of the great continental marques, the XK-SS embodies the race-proved qualities of performance, roadability, reliability and safety that Jaguar believes are as desirable on the highway as they are necessary on the track.

262 H.P. "XK" engine, 3 Weber dual carburetors, four-wheel Dunlop disc brakes, all-weather top, chrome luggage rack, full touring equipment.

JAGUAR
FIRST·FINEST
FASTEST

Jaguar
pride in its vast pa
Island City, New
from all the major
this tremendous
parts service to
North American

LEFT *Different styles of cheap US range literature, from posed studio photographs through monotone die-cuts to exterior images with animals.*

BELOW *This pretty and now rare small range brochure from 1953 used hand-coloured photography with a good amount of information and an attractive cover.*

This 1955 range brochure carries some interesting imagery showing that the rear compartment of an XK140 will accommodate people. It may have been intended for the US as well as the European market.

THE NEW 1955
JAGUAR

THE ROADSTER 2-SEATER
The most widely known and the most highly esteemed sports car in the world. Now, with higher performance, increased leg room and greater luggage accommodation, it is more than ever the aristocrat of open sports cars.

THE 2-3 SEATER HARDTOP
This entirely new model offers accommodation for three adults or two adults and two children, and has ample luggage accommodation.

THE SPORTS CAR WITH INTER

By victory after victory on the racetracks of the world, Jaguar has gained for itself a position in the very forefront of modern sports cars. Twice winners at Le Mans, three times victors at Rheims, twice winners of the R.A.C. Tourist Trophy and victorious in innumerable other International and National events, the race track breeding of Jaguar is evident from the moment the wheel is handled. All the accumulated wealth of knowledge and experience gained in the hard school of racing ·have been built into new Jaguar XK 140 models which are powered by the famous 3½ litre twin overhead camshaft XK engine, now with high lift cams and its power output

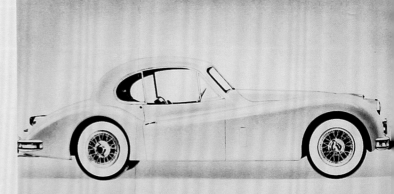

Jaguar'), and the last issue, which covered the Mark IX, showed an XK150 with cutaway rear spats and the XKSS (the only time this model was featured in literature). Others used proper photographs of the cars.

British range brochures from this period also took on different formats, from at one extreme a quite substantial and high quality mini-brochure produced in about 1953, through to single folded sheets in varying sizes.

Conclusion

This had been a mixed decade for Jaguar marketing, but a raft of new models, greater sales at home and abroad, a knighthood for Sir William Lyons, and fantastic competition successes were all good reasons why they didn't need to put the same emphasis into brochure material at this time.

NAL RACETRACK BREEDING

ed to 190 b.h.p. The increase in power of these engines coupled the introduction of rack and pinion steering provides a new high of road performance, yet, notwithstanding the high speed ntial of the XK 140, the Jaguar characteristics of smoothness, ce, tractability and road adhesion are such that complete and rtless mastery is in the hands of the driver at all times and at speeds. On all XK models, seating accommodation has been eased and extra accommodation for children is now available both the Convertible and Hardtop — the latter also affording mmodation for a third adult.

MORE LUGGAGE ROOM TOO

Not only is greatly increased luggage accommodation provided in all the new more powerful 1955 Jaguar XK models, but there is additional seating accommodation too in the Convertible and Hardtop. The Convertible is fitted with rear seats to carry two children, whilst in the Hardtop, provision is made for carrying either two children or a third adult passenger.

THE CONVERTIBLE

With all the luxury and comfort of a fully enclosed car, and with extra seating accommodation for two children, this model can be converted to an open car in an instant without leaving the seat.

The Swinging Sixties

We are now entering a very interesting decade for Jaguar: a period of expansion for the company, for its range of models, and for its new car sales resulting in a feeling of great prosperity. Effectively Jaguar started the 1960s with a clean sheet, and it was the Mark 2 – actually announced at the end of 1959 – that heralded a whole new range of models.

BELOW *Two versions of the original Mark 2 brochure with its clean and simple front cover treatment, a theme that was followed through on other models in the early 1960s. Even the later Mark 2 card folder used a simple front cover theme, but by then on a black background.*

The identification for the new car, Mark 2, was something of an anomaly because the cars it replaced, the 2.4 and 3.4-litre compact saloons, were never known at that time as the Mark 1. But the changes that took place in the Mark 2 were considered so significant that it warranted a completely new prestige brochure to show that it was an entirely new car.

For its launch at the 1959 Motor Show there was a lavish brochure, only the second from Jaguar to be spiral bound, which meant that you could fold the pages back on themselves without fear of destroying the brochure in the process. It had a new-look cover, plain, high gloss, and simple in its design, just as the black pre-war Jaguar brochure had been. Inside was quality art

paper, varnished and all printed in full colour. Although Jaguar, like many other manufacturers, were moving away from highly detailed artistic representations of the cars, this brochure displayed a mix of professional photography but with artists' work still used for detail images such as the dashboard and boot areas.

The brochure was therefore a watershed in the development of post-war Jaguar promotional literature. It was to almost the same standard as the Mark V brochure covered in the opening chapter, with better images, and of very sturdy construction – which is why so many have survived to this day. This was also a global brochure, easily adaptable to all markets. It was reprinted several times in the 1960s with some

changes but was the only brochure for the Mark 2 range for most of the car's life, although some of the photographs were reprinted as separate sheets with the technical specifications on the reverse. Later in the 1960s the brochure was supplanted by a simple card folder updating the information and with a single picture of the car.

To give the Mark 2 an extended lease of life Jaguar opted to revitalise the model while at the same time bringing down costs. This in Jaguar's eyes justified a change of name to 240 and 340 (referring to their respective engine sizes), and, therefore, the issuing of a new brochure. In hindsight the costs of this brochure must have been high in relation to the actual number of cars sold and the length of time they were in production – a mere 12 months for the larger-engined car and 18 months for the 240.

When these 'new' models were launched in September 1967, the promotional material initially took the form of a folder of the same size and style as the later Mark 2 version. This covered both models, showing the cars against aircraft backdrops. The same folder was subsequently reproduced in a cheaper form for use as a giveaway at the British Motor Show. An interesting point is that there was a spelling mistake in the folder, which spelt the word 'accommodation' with only one 'm'.

Shortly afterwards the style of and the images from the folder were reproduced in a more prestigious 12-page brochure, which used the

BELOW *The cost of a prestige launch brochure inevitably meant recycling some content, such as this picture of a Mark 2, originally in maroon in 1961, but retouched in white (without the whitewall tyres) for the late 1960s card folder.*

BOTTOM *Still using some artists' work even in the 1960s, the Mark 2 brochure was the first to use this type of treatment for the dashboard layout – almost what you would associate with a drivers' handbook rather than promotional material.*

RIGHT *Expensive and extensive material for models only in production for a very limited period. Similar treatment was also adopted for the later Daimler V8 250 model.*

BELOW *The well-known ship/captain image was used extensively to promote the 240 and 340 models, with the plates changed according to model.*

same image on its front cover. By virtue of its size this brochure was able to cover the attributes of the 240 and 340 in far more detail, with the addition of some other interesting pictures, not least a full-colour image of a 240 at the dockside alongside a ship with the obligatory smartly dressed captain in control. Could it be that Jaguar were taking a leaf out of the Armstrong Siddeley brochures of the 1950s, when they did much the same with their Sapphire model?

This luxurious brochure for what were then the cheapest models in the Jaguar range was short-lived, because the 340 was dropped the following September. This necessitated the production of a new version for the 240 alone, a highly unusual procedure for a model that was also destined for a short production run that lasted only until 1969 – probably the only time in the history of the Jaguar marque (thus far) that a short-lived model has enjoyed such publicity.

The Daimler V8 connection

Daimler, the oldest surviving British car manufacturer, became part of the Jaguar group in 1960, and the cars that Jaguar inherited at

BELOW _Daimler were decidedly behind the times with their SP250 promotional material, reminiscent of the sort of thing you might find for an MGA in the mid-1950s._

BUILT TO GO PLACES... _FAST!_

People who're going places . . . fast . . are going Daimler SP.250! Nimble as a kitten in town traffic, yet the motorway is the true domain of the SP.250. To feel its eager response as you open up is to know a new motoring adventure. And with the exhilaration of its power you get the confidence of feather-light handling, positive disc-braking and impeccable cornering.

Breathtaking as its performance is SP.250 styling! From sleek, fluted grill to flaunting rear fins, every eye-appealing curve of its body expresses the spirit of speed.

This, then is the SP.250, the newest and most exciting of all fine sports cars. A car that will captivate the newcomer as surely as the seasoned driver. A car that is a joy to drive and a source of never ending, thrilling satisfaction.

For performance . . . styling . . . handling . . . go Daimler SP.250!

Daimler V8 S.P. 250

BY APPOINTMENT
TO H.M. QUEEN ELIZABETH THE QUEEN MOTHER
MOTOR CAR MANUFACTURERS
THE DAIMLER COMPANY LTD.

DAIMLER 3·8

We present the Daimler MAJESTIC—a luxury car with a dual personality, its character changing to match your mood of the moment. On great—and small—occasions, this spacious saloon glistens with all the dignity and grandeur of its name. Docile and alert it glides through city traffic without apparent effort precision-driven by automatic transmission. You arrive at your engagement, clothes and nerves unruffled—consciously grateful for that added touch of confidence.

On the open road, the temperament of the MAJESTIC varies with your will. Should you wish for speed . . . up to 100 m.p.h. . . . the car is eager to obey. Elegance becomes sleekness as you unleash the potent 3.8 litre engine. Magnificent suspension and roadholding invites fast, safe cornering. And, at all times, those fabulous disc brakes are poised—equally responsive to the touch of caution or the slash of urgency.

MOTORING

ERN MANNER

impeccable appearance and perfect manners, the
gh performance to an extent which offers new
V-type 8-cylinder engine delivers its tremendous
e of flexibility which is truly remarkable.

command, the Majestic Major is supremely safe,
ich are fitted on all four wheels. Power-assisted
befits its famous marque and providing refined
on a new meaning when one owns a Majestic

ABOVE *An interesting comparison between the six-cylinder Daimler Majestic material produced by the traditional Daimler company and the later Majestic Major equivalent from Jaguar Cars. Although there are many similarities, the 'at speed on the road' picture is clearly penned by the same artists as the front cover of the Mark IX brochure covered in the previous chapter. The Daimler side-on view is very traditional and similar views can be found in most 1940s and 1950s Daimler material.*

that time – the SP250 sports and the Majestic saloon, latterly the Majestic Major – cannot be ignored.

The sports car was an unusual vehicle in many ways that never quite made the impact the company intended, as a last ditch attempt, more or less, to produce a competitive vehicle. Right from the start William Lyons of Jaguar realised its lack of potential, particularly when he was shortly to introduce the fabulous E-type, but, to give him credit, he persevered with the Daimler until 1964, when it was finally dropped from the range.

As for the Daimler flagship saloon, the Majestic Major, production of this car moved to the Jaguar factory in Browns Lane in 1961. Lyons himself then expanded the model range by the introduction of the DR450, a stretched limousine version that turned out to be relatively popular. These Daimlers, however, were also relatively short-lived, as both the saloon and limousine went out of production in 1967.

This brings us to the first entirely new Daimler produced by Jaguar, the 2.5-litre V8

of 1962. Using the Jaguar Mark 2 bodyshell as its base, this would turn out to be one of the more popular Daimler models up to that time.

The traditional Daimler market was somewhat under-stated and conservative, as exemplified by the term 'old money'. Whilst Jaguar catered for a, typically, slightly younger, sportier market, the Daimler 2.5-litre V8 aimed at more established steady drivers, such as solicitors and doctors, so the brochure produced for this car was, quite rightly, different from the usual Jaguar material, though still surprisingly innovative for this market.

Not just a mere folder but produced in envelope style, the opening flap incorporated a seal in the form of a silver foil Daimler radiator grille. Opening it up revealed a split page showing an overhead view of the car at speed; opened up again it revealed a full-colour image of the car with side flaps featuring details (the dashboard picture was retouched from the Jaguar Mark 2 brochure).

Although certainly not as prestigious as the original Jaguar Mark 2 offering, the Daimler item did fit nicely within the range of material available in the mid-1960s. It was reprinted in 1964, when money was saved by using lower-quality paper and omitting the foil seal.

The trend set by the Mark 2 in the mid-1960s with trim and name changes also occurred with the Daimler, which now became the V8 250. A conventional eight-page brochure was produced like that of the Jaguar, and was also accompanied by a folder, likewise in the same format as for the Jaguar.

The E-type 'GT'

Following in chronological order, the next entirely new model was the E-type introduced in March 1961, which was the most important car to come out of the company before 1968. It may never have been able to match the sales of the Mark 2, yet it became an instant icon of the period and has remained so ever since.

Continuing the new 'house style' established with the Mark 2, the same promotional approach was used for the E-type, and this makes a fascinating comparison with the XK120, the equivalent model from over a decade earlier.

The XK, for example, was not well planned, with full-scale production never being the aim. In contrast, more development was put into the E-type and it was always intended to be a full production sports car. Similarly a confused publicity decision meant that the XK originally shared a brochure with a saloon, and even when it did get its own brochure it wasn't significant and there was still confusion over whether it would be launched as a two-model range.

BELOW *Unusual treatment for the early 1960s Daimler version of Jaguar promotional material – in some ways not as prestigious, but in others more innovative.*

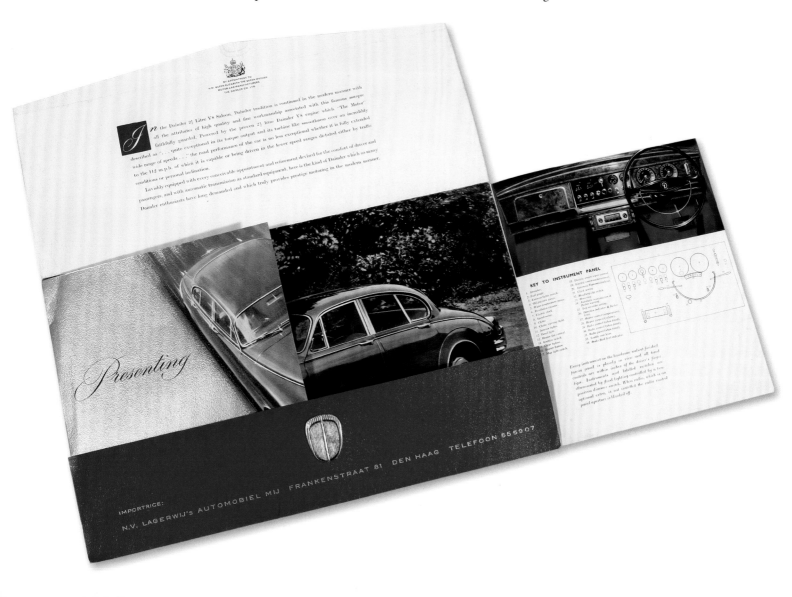

BELOW *The unique approach of attractive studio photographs, hand-finished with sky backdrops, was only used for the E-type brochure in the 1960s, although a similar treatment had been used back in 1938. Another unusual feature was that not only were the Roadster and Fixed Head models covered, but the GT – shown here with its hard top fitted (an optional extra) – was also given the same prominence.*

For the E-type it was very different, with clear decisions regarding the range of models and a pre-planned strategy for its launch and promotional material.

Also, despite being aimed at the same market, the XK had to fight for its position, as Jaguar had little sports car experience at that time. By the time the E-type was launched they had a past record both in sports car sales and competition success.

Therefore it is fair to say that the launch brochure for the E-type centred on selling the car to an expanding market of drivers not only interested in outright performance, but who also wanted fast, comfortable motoring with an image – Grand Touring, in fact – as confirmed in the launch brochure.

For this brochure the cover was dominated by an image of the E-type's three-spoked, wood-rimmed steering wheel, an image that would stay with the car throughout its production. The first page introduction, understated, covered the racing pedigree of the marque, with a discrete chequered flag at the bottom and even more discrete use of circuit and competition names set into the background.

The emphasis was, however, on 'Grand Touring', 'Elegant', and 'Luxuriously Appointed' – not what you might have expected for a new 150mph sports car! The words 'GT' seemed to be trying to deliberately distance this car from the norm of a rakish, noisy sports car.

Jaguar had always maintained a close relationship with the British *Autocar* and *Motor*

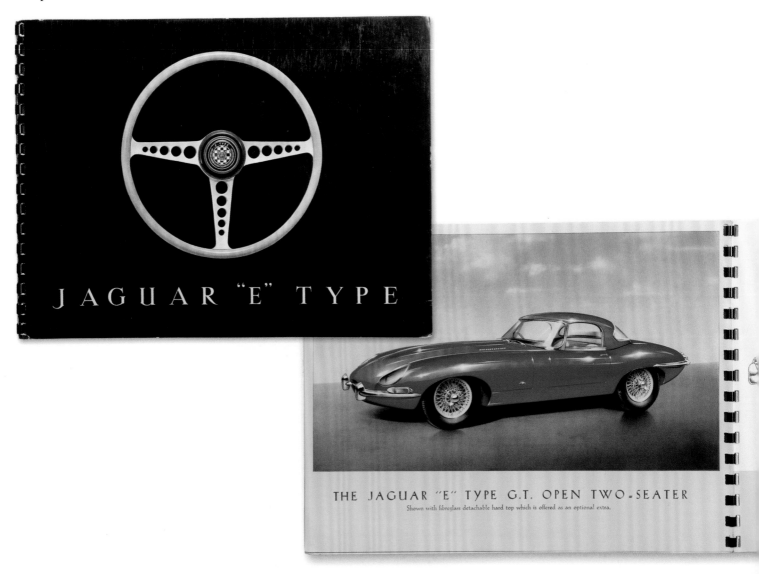

magazines, and on this occasion contributions from both featured in the brochure with road test information and cutaway drawings.

This prestigious brochure was reprinted at least twice, on the latter occasion with different spiral binding, but all are otherwise identical as the car remained virtually unchanged until the introduction of the 4.2-litre models in 1964.

With the superb world response to the E-type, and despite the advancements made in 1964, the revised 4.2 only warranted a simple card folder, again in the house style of the period like the later Mark 2. This time, however, there was a stunning bright red cover and, inside, a return to an artistic impression of a red car at speed. Interestingly the original 'GT' designation given to the E-type in 1961 was now dropped!

No other material specifically for the E-type was produced until 1966, when Jaguar introduced a new (additional) model, the 2+2. By this time the 'house style' had moved on to a less substantial brochure, though of the same size as before but with a stark white cover. For the E-type this was a 2+2 brochure only, and there was a strange mix of artwork and photography inside. This brochure was reprinted in 1967 to take account of exterior styling changes (exposed headlights), and the opportunity was taken to publish new colour pictures inside, an easy and inexpensive option because the car would soon be replaced by the Series 2 model anyway.

For the Series 2 brochure (or folder) Jaguar amalgamated the models into just one

LEFT *Changing front cover styles for E-type brochures in the mid-1960s.*

FAR RIGHT *Keeping costs down: although printed to meet the changes in style from Series 1 to Series 1½ models, the blue car in the harbour scene is still a Series 1!*

RIGHT *This folder was the only promotional item produced in the UK for the Series 2. It was poorly printed and was the first time the BL logo appeared, although there was no mention of the Group anywhere.*

publication, an unusual concertina affair, poorly printed and with very unusual front cover treatment. This was obviously intended for worldwide use as all the cars featured side repeater lights, a standard fitment for the US market. The whole presentation was not up to previous standards and the most striking aspect was the British Leyland logo on the opening page, the very first time it had appeared on a Jaguar brochure but certainly not the last!

A new flagship model – the Mark X saloon

The third entirely new offering from Jaguar at the start of the 1960s was the Mark X, the flagship saloon that replaced the aged Mark VII to IX design. For some reason, rather than go for a 'corporate' look from the outset with the nice gloss spiral-bound quality look, Jaguar opted for a Daimler V8 style folder. Quite large in size and predominantly dark blue, this

BELOW *A comparison of imagery from the Series 1 and Series 1½ 2+2 E-type brochures. The yellow car is obviously artistically stretched to create a roomy appearance inside, while the setting for the red car seems totally out of context. Would you collect logs in an E-type?*

65

LEFT *The earlier larger format folder and the proper early brochure for the Mark X. Jaguar seemed undecided on what to actually call the model at this time!*

LEFT *The painting of the Mark X in the first folder is another example of early published material being based on a pre-production car (it doesn't have the production model rear lighting treatment).*

JAGUAR MARK TEN

JAGUAR MARK X

Luxury and Refinement in the True Jaguar Tradition

This comprehensive view of the spacious interior shows the luxurious accommodation provided for five adults whose every comfort has been carefully studied. Upholstery is in finest quality Vaumol leather hide over deep Dunlopillo foam rubber cushions. Centre folding arm rests are fitted in both front and rear compartments — deep pile carpets are fitted throughout. A comprehensive range of instruments together with a row of clearly labelled switches are mounted in a handsome figured-walnut panel. A glove compartment — with lock and interior light — and a full width shelf provide ample accommodation for personal effects. A completely new high-efficiency heating and ventilating system is provided with individual controls for each side of the car as well as a separate delivery system to the rear compartment.

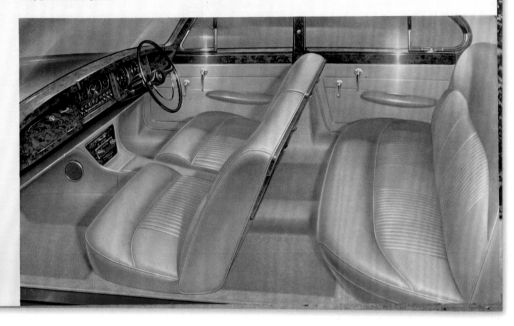

LEFT *Layout of the prestige Mark X brochure was similar to those of the E-type and Mark 2, but the full-colour interior painting had ideas copied from 1950s Daimler material.*

BELOW LEFT *Stunning full-page bled-off images of the car did the Mark X proud. This example, often retouched in different colours for other promotional advertising, is set against Sir William Lyons's home in Warwickshire.*

The
MARK TEN JAGUAR

RIGHT and **BELOW**
The effective front cover treatment belied what lay inside. The painting emphasises the bulbous styling of the Mark X.

envelope-style pre-launch folder employed a growler silver foil seal, and the opening flaps (this time with a Jaguar leaper on them) revealed a painting of a Mark X against a country garden backdrop. For this model Jaguar adapted the earlier slogan 'Grace…Space…and Pace' into 'New Grace…New Space…and New Pace'.

In contrast, the quality launch folder followed house practice, though its midnight blue cover incorporated the embossed foil growler badge. Confusion obviously ruled here, as it has done so many times in Jaguar promotional material: whereas on the first folder (described above) the front cover title was 'Jaguar Mark X', on the lavish brochure it was 'Jaguar Mark Ten'!

Another interesting observation is that the E-type was the first car to appear with the new independent rear suspension, and its early launch in March of that year should have proved a better platform from which to trumpet its attributes; yet it has scant coverage in the E-type brochure and no illustration. But in the Mark X folder it gets not only a full page, but also a full-colour cutaway of the arrangement.

This brochure was reprinted during 1962/3 in the same covers, but with the specifications updated and some images replaced.

When the model was upgraded to the 4.2-litre version in 1964 the 'new' folder followed the house style of the other two cars and adopted a striking cover image of the front portion of the car. Inside it was a return to artwork with a Mark X on the road at speed.

Less than a year later, perhaps due to the poor sales response to the Mark X, another prestigious brochure was produced. This was of 12 pages again, printed on quality art paper, with varnished covers and spiral binding. A completely new set of pictures was created for this brochure, with cars in gold, green, maroon, pastel blue and even white (not a good colour for the Mark X!), plus no less than eight full-colour images of various mechanical components. This brochure was one of the first to feature people with the car, something which would become more popular as the years went by.

It was unusual, considering the poor sales of the Mark X over the years, that so much material should have been produced. Either this was because of the poor sales (ie in the hope of generating more), or because it was the company's flagship saloon and was therefore considered deserving of such treatment. We shall never know.

BELOW *Exceptionally poor quality production for what was the most expensive and prestigious limousine model in the Jaguar range at the time. The title on the front cover and the car were retouched to produce the 420G equivalent leaflet.*

BELOW BOTTOM *Wide-angle studio photography using a dark-coloured car didn't enhance the presentation of the new 420G model.*

A well designed and executed brochure for the 420G. Measuring only 6in x 7¹/₂in (152mm x 190mm), it deserved to be produced in a much larger size to give it more impact. The first opening revealed the complete interior across two pages.

Opening it up again revealed a very clear, wide image of the dashboard across the next two pages.

A rare sight of a two-tone paint finish 420G, the only time that one was depicted in a UK brochure.

Your car Sir!

The Jaguar 420G – the car built around the company director.

Sink into your elegant seat. Stretch out your legs. Give the word to your chauffeur. And glide noiselessly away.

Your first sensation is one of space. More than enough room for five large-size adults. And more than enough room for their brief-cases, umbrellas, hats and other impedimenta.

Then examine the comfort of your surroundings. Armrests, picnic-tables, carpets, ventilation. All designed to put you at your ease. And if privacy is as important as comfort there's a limousine version with a sliding glass partition. We know you company directors like to keep your secrets.

Specification

ENGINE. Six cylinder 4.2 litre XK engine with twin overhead camshafts and three carburetters. 92·07 mm. bore x 106 mm. stroke. Capacity 4,235 c.c. 255 b.h.p. at 5,400 r.p.m. Compression ratio 8 to 1. Cooling system incorporates cross-flow tube and fin radiator block, fluid drive speed-control fan and improved design water pump

TRANSMISSION. (Manual) Four-speed all-synchromesh gearbox gear change lever on floor between front seats. (Overdrive) As above with addition of a Laycock de Normanville overdrive controlled by lever on steering column. (Automatic) Borg Warner automatic transmission with dual drive range D1/D2. Selector lever on steering column

SUSPENSION. (Front) Independent suspension – double wishbones, coil springs with telescopic shock absorbers. (Rear) Fully independent suspension incorporating on each side: a lower transverse link pivoted at wheel carrier and subframe adjacent to differential case and, above this, a half-shaft universally jointed at each end. Twin coil springs each enclose a telescopic hydraulic damper

BRAKES. Servo-assisted disc brakes all round. Independent hydraulic circuits to front and rear. Self adjusting handbrake

STEERING. 'Varamatic' variable ratio power steering. 2·75 turns lock to lock

WHEELS & TYRES. Pressed steel bolt-on disc wheels. Dunlop 205 mm. × 14 in. RS5 tyres and tubes

FUEL SUPPLY. Twin tanks, total capacity 20 gallons. Twin electric pumps. Separate concealed fillers. Change-over switch on facia panel

ELECTRICAL EQUIPMENT & INSTRUMENTS. Alternator generator. 12-volt battery with negative earth system. Extensive equipment includes – Four headlamp system with headlamp flashing unit, twin reversing lamps, map reading lamp, continuous side winkers, cigar lighter, twin-blade two-speed windscreen wipers, windscreen washers, automatic ignition advance, transistorised clock, all fitted as standard. Comprehensive instrumentation to Jaguar normal high standards

BODY. All steel four-door five-seater saloon. Luxurious upholstery in ventilated leather hide over deep Dunlopillo cushions. Central folding armrests front and rear. Reclining front seats with flush fitting picnic trays in backs of squabs. Deep pile carpets over thick felt underlay. Padded safety screen rail. 27 cubic feet capacity luggage boot

HEATING & DEMISTING. High output system. Regulation for temperature, volume and direction of air for each side of saloon. Separate ducting to rear compartment

SPARE WHEEL & TOOLS. Spare wheel housed in luggage boot and fully trimmed to protect luggage. Comprehensive set of tools in special container

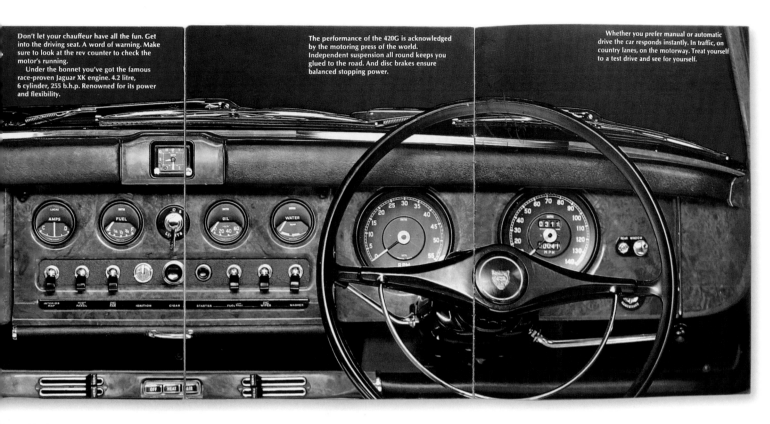

Don't let your chauffeur have all the fun. Get into the driving seat. A word of warning. Make sure to look at the rev counter to check the motor's running.

Under the bonnet you've got the famous race-proven Jaguar XK engine. 4.2 litre, 6 cylinder, 255 b.h.p. Renowned for its power and flexibility.

The performance of the 420G is acknowledged by the motoring press of the world. Independent suspension all round keeps you glued to the road. And disc brakes ensure balanced stopping power.

Whether you prefer manual or automatic drive the car responds instantly. In traffic, on country lanes, on the motorway. Treat yourself to a test drive and see for yourself.

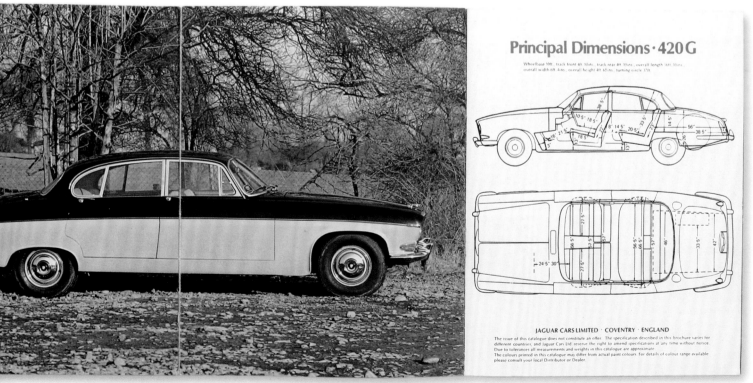

Principal Dimensions · 420G

Wheelbase 10ft., track front 4ft. 10ins., track rear 4ft. 10ins., overall length 16ft. 10ins., overall width 6ft. 4ins., overall height 4ft. 6½ins., turning circle 37ft.

JAGUAR CARS LIMITED · COVENTRY · ENGLAND

BELOW *Acetate overlays have been used before and since, but I doubt that they've ever again been used with such ingenuity as in this US launch material for the Mark X. The door has an acetate window through which you are tempted to view the interior…*

…And lifting the page reveals the inside of the door and the full interior.

Jaguar, however, persevered with the Mark X design, redesignating it the 420G in 1967 at the same time as the other ranges were rationalised. Unlike the Mark 2 the 420G wasn't cheapened, although aspects of its trim were altered and prices were reduced. Another new brochure – smaller, with different cover and pictures – was also produced, but again did little for the car.

An oddity was the production of a poor quality flimsy leaflet to promote the sale of the limousine version. It is obvious that Jaguar never expected to sell many of these cars, and the leaflet did little to promote them either.

Another unusual item was the production of a 420G brochure in the form of a multi-page colour brochure with the tempting picture of a rear door on the cover. Opening it revealed the full interior and again showed several well executed split-page images, a unique Jaguar British approach that seems never to have been repeated. It is also unique in depicting a two-tone exterior paint finished 420G for the home market.

These represented the only unique offerings for the Mark X and 420G, although in the US Jaguar Cars Inc produced what must have been their most lavish presentation for a Jaguar in that country, anticipating huge sales for the car. Supplied in a white envelope embossed with the name Jaguar, the white brochure inside echoed

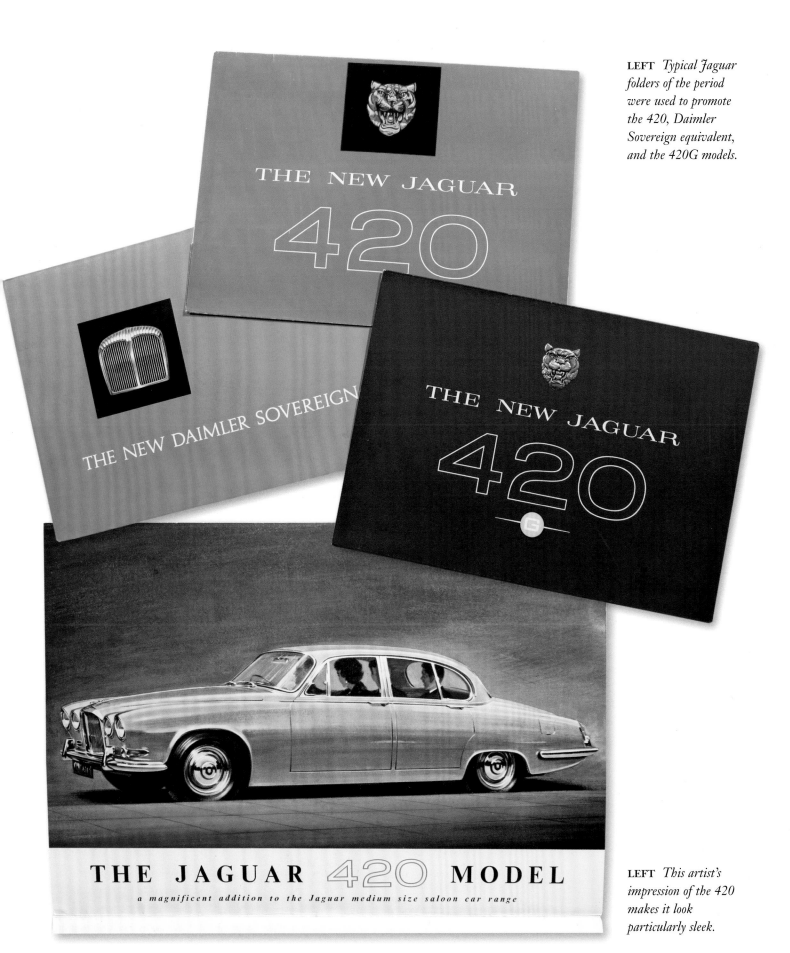

THE NEW JAGUAR 420

THE NEW DAIMLER SOVEREIGN

THE NEW JAGUAR 420 G

THE JAGUAR 420 MODEL

a magnificent addition to the Jaguar medium size saloon car range

LEFT *Typical Jaguar folders of the period were used to promote the 420, Daimler Sovereign equivalent, and the 420G models.*

LEFT *This artist's impression of the 420 makes it look particularly sleek.*

BELOW *The front cover of the combined 420 and 420G brochure produced in 1967. Of the same format as other brochures of the period, the cover treatment is unique and quite contemporary and attractive for Jaguar at the time.*

the same approach. The full-colour content included real photographs of the car, two pages on Coventry with an aerial photograph, two pages on the heritage of the marque, and then the stunning addition of acetate overlays, one showing the chassis structure against the bodywork in colour while the other is best explained by viewing the accompanying pictures. A fabulous presentation and well worthy of special mention. It is only a pity that the car didn't live up to this treatment, as sales were very disappointing.

420 – Daimler Sovereign

At this point, although strictly out of chronological order, we ought to bring in the

420 models, because their promotion was incorporated with that of the 420G model at a later stage. Eager to continue expanding its market share, yet another new model, the 420, came out in 1966. Although it inevitably had a short shelf-life this model also appeared as the company's first truly badge-engined Daimler, the Sovereign.

Because of its anticipated short lifespan the 420 never benefited from prestigious brochures but started out with a simple folder in the house style of Jaguar's other models. Inside the artist had been hard at work as usual, stretching the perspective to make the car look longer and lower than it actually was! A Daimler Sovereign version looked visually more appealing but the text was virtually the same.

Both a prestige brochure and a folder were later reprinted for the Daimler Sovereign, but the Jaguar had to share its brochure with the 420G. This made for quite an attractive chunky brochure, although the best part of it was the front cover.

S-type saloons

Going back now to 1963, the Jaguar range expanded again with another new model, the S-type – or 'S' Type as Jaguar always referred to it in their publicity material at the time. A halfway house in terms of prestige and financial value between the sporting Mark 2 and the gargantuan Mark X, in Jaguar's eyes this made it worthy of separate promotion. Probably

produced for the 1963 motor shows, a magazine format brochure was published providing detailed information, with an attractive maroon car featured on the front cover against a harbour background. The title read 'Introducing the Jaguar 3.4 and 3.8 'S'. An interesting point is that the text referred to 'the salient features', an expression that Jaguar copywriters hadn't used since the days of the XK120. Finally, on this item, at the rear a golden sand 'S' Type was shown against a rocky beach background – but unfortunately the car appears to have had a repaint at the rear and the finish doesn't match! A less than unique example of lack of attention to detail in the Lyons era. It is also worth noting that a very similar form of magazine promotion was used at the time for the launch of the Rover 2000.

BELOW *Probably the nicest picture taken of a 420, unusually from the rear three-quarter viewpoint. The nicely lit studio pose does the car justice.*

Initially a simple card folder was produced, later followed by a full-size, house style spiral-bound brochure but with another different cover image. The fact that it contains a reference to the car being voted the 1963 New York Motor Show Car of 1964 indicates that this brochure wasn't produced until after the launch. The colour photographs inside were very life-style and business-like, posed against modern sculptures, the Houses of Parliament, and even Buckingham Palace – a distinct change to what had gone before, indicating a change in marketing approach.

Following Jaguar practice at the time, for the later reprint the style of brochure changed to the plain white cover variety and the internal pictures were retaken to cover such subtle model changes as the style of hubcap. Though this had fewer pages and a more basic layout, the S-type was still depicted in a business environment against a modern office block.

Range brochures

As far as the models covered in this chapter are concerned, range brochures took on a new

LEFT _What could have been well-produced colour photographs for the S-type were marred. This hand-coloured photograph of a car has been superimposed on the Buckingham Palace background, giving it a false look – not least because, despite being in the middle of the road, there is no driver!_

BELOW _A wide choice of handout material available in the 1960s, from UK-based material with press shots to US artistry that didn't show the cars off to their best advantage._

RIGHT and **BELOW**
*Unusual for Jaguar
brochures up to this
time was the use of an
overseas backdrop with
a foreign-registered car.
The later black brochure
incorporates details and
photographs of both the
outgoing 420G model
and its replacement, the
2.8/4.2-litre XJ6.*

importance during the 1960s. A wider range of cars and expansion of sales justified a greater emphasis in this area, with more 'giveaways' for motor shows and showrooms.

Very smart but attractive smaller range brochures were produced throughout this period, featuring all the models and regularly updated. These used the concertina format, were in full colour, and a nice touch on the front cover of the early examples were the words 'With the Compliments of…' Similar offerings (of slightly different dimensions) were offered in the States, but mostly used uninspiring artwork.

Alongside the small folders, Jaguar also produced larger range material. For example, in 1967 a standard-size landscape brochure featured a very stylish front cover with chromed leaper artwork against a striking sky, an image often used by Jaguar in magazine advertising. Inside, each car had a two-page spread comprising a full-page colour image facing a page of specifications and black and white interior.

There were also smaller 6in x 9in (152mm x 229mm) booklet-style brochures depicting all the models made at the time. Published in 1967 with a white cover and republished in 1968 in black, these provide an interesting account of all the models available at those dates. Interestingly the later issue is the only brochure to feature the XJ6 and 420G together.

By contrast Jaguar in North America produced some lavish brochures, although they always seemed to suffer from poor photograph reproduction.

Oddballs

During this period Jaguar produced various editions of a 'Case Book', a unique insight into Jaguar history and its development over the years, instigated by the late Andrew Whyte, Jaguar PR man and later independent historian. These represent an excellent account of the cars, the company and its many acquisitions over the years, and were also the first publications to make extensive use of archive

BELOW *This 1961 US range brochure seems to be high quality and was produced in two sizes, but the print quality is poor and one has to question some of the backdrops!*

BELOW *Some lovely artwork was used by Jaguar to promote their cars on the front covers of British car magazines in the 1960s – the last time we were to see such treatment.*

material held by the company. Initially produced in the mid-1960s, the book was reprinted several times with different covers – to my knowledge four times – and remains an excellent reference work to this day. Daimler-specific versions also became available much later.

A similar but even more prestigious book was published to commemorate the company's 50th anniversary (1922 to 1972). With a hard cover showing a blue XJ6 Series 1, this very pleasant publication was made available to some first-in-line XJ12 owners in 1972.

All these booklets were available for purchase by dealers to be used as giveaways to 'good' customers. They were also used for other

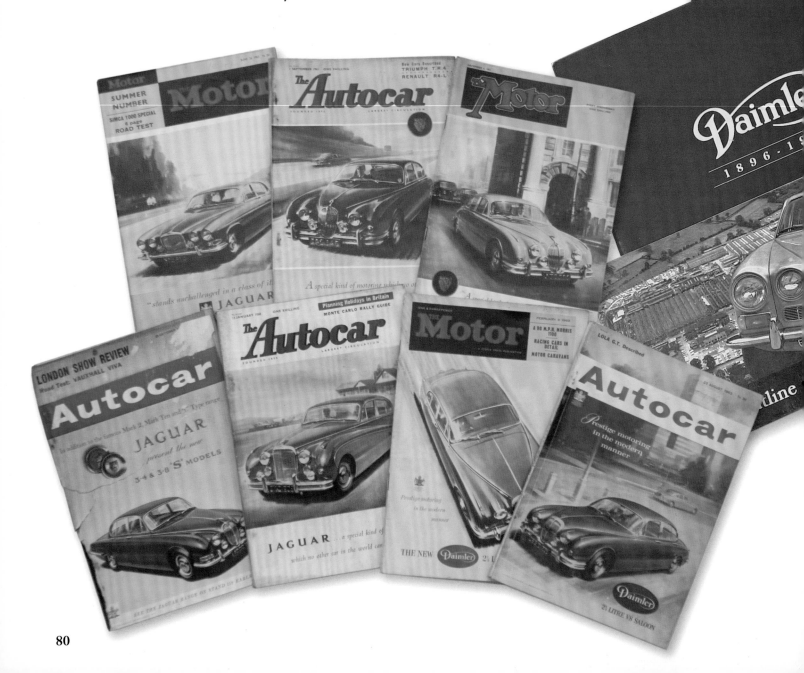

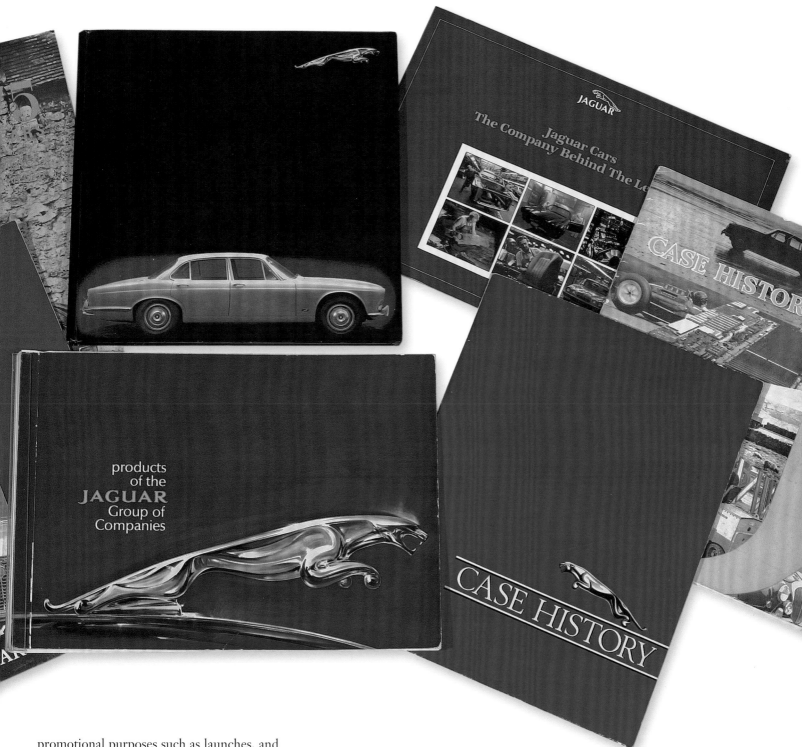

promotional purposes such as launches, and were even sent out by the factory, on request, to the general public.

This brings to an end the very busy 1960s, for Jaguar an era of model expansion and finally contraction, which witnessed the emergence of a more corporate identity behind its promotional material and presentation but also saw the start of British Leyland intervention, of which more was to follow.

ABOVE *Examples of the various 'Case Book' publications and other, later varieties of promotional booklets produced by Jaguar Cars.*

THE NEW SOVEREIGN, BY DAIMLER

Daimler Sove

Aspects of the new

DAIMLER SOVEREIGN

The JAGUAR
Four-Door Saloon Car Range.
XJ 3·4, 4·2 and 5·3

Allegr
1100/1300

GENESIS OF THE

JAGUAR XJ6

VORWORT

INTRODUCTION

BESCHREIE

FORSCHUN
ENTWURT

DESCRIPTION

RECHERCHES ET
CONSTRUCTION

JAGUAR XJ6

JAGUAR

Daimler Lim

SERI

JAG

JAG

IES 3
TYPE

JAGUAR

The British Leyland era

We now move into a very different era for the company, during which, under the control of British Leyland, there were many changes, most of which would be to the detriment of Jaguar and would affect the promotional material produced.

BELOW *Rather dull covers for the launch brochure and folder relating to the E-type Series 3, a major new car and the first car to carry the V12 engine!*

The promotional material moved away from stylised drawings and paintings completely, and turned to professional photography in a variety of location settings. However, the word 'professional' has to be taken lightly in some cases, since this was a time of integration and it was not unusual to find a BL photographer working with Leyland commercial products one day and given an assignment to photograph a prestige Daimler on the next. This shows through clearly in some of the work produced. Overall, the quality of the items produced was confused and substandard during this period, with a wide range of paper stock being used and little sense of direction or, sometimes, appreciation of what the typical Jaguar or Daimler customer was looking for in a car.

The range brochures also reflected the BL 'influence'. For example it was normal to find an extensive booklet format being used promoting everything from an Austin Mini through to a Daimler limousine, the sort of promotional material common to the likes of Ford and Vauxhall in the 1970s and 1980s but not right for Jaguar.

The end for the E-type

Starting with one of the last of the traditional Jaguars, the final fling for the ageing E-type was in Series 3 form with V12 engine, the first production car to feature this unit. Promotional literature for the car appeared in March 1971 in the form of a folder plus a full catalogue. Predominantly black, the cover ironically provided no evidence of the car incorporating the brand new V12 engine, perhaps because this was another case of material pre-empting actual

LEFT *An obviously hurried publication with lack of attention to detail and ill-conceived backdrops such as the inner-Coventry slip road. The Kenilworth Castle picture is as bad, and the lighting is not good.*

production. Inside were photographs of an XK-engined car as well as the V12, the former never offered for sale. Intended as a global brochure, it was printed in four languages.

This was an entirely new style of brochure, as the copywriters themselves pointed out in the first paragraph: 'For an E-type with a difference, a catalogue which is different.' The images took the form of a scrapbook format, disjointed, covering a variety of locations from Coventry concrete jungle and Kenilworth Castle (complete with scaffolding), to a lady dressed like Little Red Riding Hood! This style appears never to have been used again so was probably found not to be to anyone's liking at the time. Hardly enticing

material for an exciting new V12 sports car, but it represents the only European offering for this model, although it was reprinted around 1973 on textured paper with references to the XK-engined version deleted.

In contrast to the poor European offering the US equivalent was a far more interesting affair, with a particularly good cover showing a car behind wrought iron gates, the copy reading 'Jaguar unlocks the ultimate cat'. The cover splits into two halves (like the 420G brochure in the last chapter), so that the gates open to reveal the car in all its glory, captioned as 'The V12 animal'. Overall a much better offering, with good photography throughout.

ABOVE The layout is also disjointed in the Series 3 brochure. The left-hand page depicts both engines, so why publish another V12 picture on the next page and why leave all that blank space?

Genesis of the Jaguar V12

An unusual and unique presentation is a very high quality brochure, prepared specifically for the launch of the V12 engine, with no connection to the cars this unit powered.

Of typical Jaguar format and size, the cover was exciting, in blood red with light dancing off engineering swarf. Inside, filing-cabinet style sections provided a wealth of information on research, design, and development, plus a separate detailed booklet with more text detail, all in three languages. The highlight has to be, however, the superb Tranart presentation of the engine, four superbly detailed full-colour acetate sheets depicting the engine in various states of build. With all four acetates in position the complete engine is depicted, and lifting each sheet individually reveals a cutaway section.

Even the reverse of each acetate sheet is true to the engine detail.

A beautifully produced and unique brochure presentation, it remains one of the finest items produced by Jaguar over the years. Either because the cost of its production was so high at the time, necessitating a huge print-run, or because the publicity gained by Jaguar issuing such a prestige brochure to all and sundry was considered worthwhile, it remains one of the most commonly seen Jaguar promotional items to this day.

Unfolding the XJ6 story

Introduced in 1968, the XJ6 was destined to become the most important model Jaguar had produced up to that time, and it led the company into a one-saloon-model policy

RIGHT *The US copywriters and brochure producers showed initiative with the presentation of the E-type Series 3.*

FAR RIGHT TOP *A stunning cover and quality presentation and lots of it make the Genesis brochure something any advertising literature enthusiast should own.*

FAR RIGHT BOTTOM *Incredibly well presented and executed, the double-sided acetate engine 'build' is worthy of any paper material produced by any manufacturer in any year.*

that lasted for many years. Initially the Jaguar influence was still there in its promotional material, even though the BL logo was present (as it was on all literature for the foreseeable future).

As one would expect, such a vital new car warranted an entirely new prestige catalogue. Of the same size as many of the 1960s offerings, the big difference was the style, which epitomised a move into modernity for Jaguar marketing. The front cover, for example, is beautifully simple yet very effective. The nose of the car, photographed low down with a starburst filter on the camera lens, spreads the light from the headlights, and above it are just the words 'Jaguar XJ6' in bold type. The cover appeared thicker than it actually was

because of a double fold opening which revealed more of the same car. To complement this, on the rear cover another photograph employed gimmickry to accentuate the motion effect of a car at speed.

Inside you were immediately invited to 'Enter the private world of the Jaguar XJ6.' The brochure (or catalogue, as they called it) enticed you to visit your Jaguar dealer and see the car in the flesh! It was the very first time such a marketing approach was taken, and the copywriters really went to town. It was published in four languages – English, French, German and Italian.

Another interesting touch is the unusual treatment of some photographs, where specifically small areas of the car are shown,

JAGUAR XJ6

LEFT *An attractive approach to launch material for the XJ6 – a stunning front cover image. The smaller item was a simple folded sheet with images taken from the big brochure, for use as an economical giveaway.*

LEFT *Opening up the front cover revealed the entire car in all its splendour, complete with glamorous lady. The reverse of the cover also incorporated a stunning side-view of a blue car.*

ABOVE *The female touch: travelling at speed and enjoying a leisurely chat with the driver – and why not paint your nails within the smooth and cosseted environment of an XJ6?*

such as a rear light unit or the radiator badge. Another first was a picture of the full interior taken side on – obviously with all the doors removed for ease of access! The only way such views had been attempted before, such as in the Mark X brochure, was by means of hand-painted artwork.

There was glamour as well with a very attractive lady soaking up the ambience of the new Jaguar. In one picture she is seen reclining in the front seat, in another delicately running her fingers over the dashboard switchgear, and in a third painting her fingernails whilst the car is driven at speed (the carefully placed nail polish resting steadily on the dash roll top!).

This brochure saw the first use of what was to become a 1970s buzzword, 'ergonomics', referring in this instance to the dashboard layout – a little ironic when some people complained that it was confusing with all the switches being of the same style.

In conclusion, this brochure was made up of no less than 44 pages, the largest ever produced up to that time. Its layout was new, appealing, and offered some unusual ideas for the time – still pre-1970s, remember. There is an irony here, in that the car sold so exceptionally well that there were long waiting lists to acquire one – so perhaps such a mammoth offering wasn't really necessary! Nevertheless, it was the only brochure produced for the Jaguar XJ6 Series 1 and lasted throughout the life of the model, being reprinted at least three times. This was facilitated by the clever approach of placing the brochure's text on separate half sheets within the main binding that could be altered easily for reprints without amending the rest of the brochure content.

The retention of the Daimler name was important to Jaguar as it encouraged a different type of customer, so a Daimler equivalent of the XJ6 was announced in October 1969. This retained the name of the outgoing model –

Sovereign – and was basically another badge engineering exercise.

After the modernistic style of the XJ6 literature, a different approach was taken for the Daimler: not so much a brochure or folder but a portfolio. A subdued varnished white folder with an embossed image of the fluted grille was all you saw. Opening the folder revealed brief information sheets and four full-colour A2 posters. Professional photographers Michael Williams, John Hedgecoe, Michael Boys, and Gerry Cranham were commissioned to provide

images that captured and expressed their appreciation of the car.

This approach was never used again but was typical of some of the unique ideas being presented in those days. It also emphasised the different image for Daimler models compared to Jaguars, so that one brand did not conflict with the other but complemented it.

Some time later an ordinary eight-page brochure was published for the Daimler Sovereign, using pictures from the same photo shoots as the poster portfolio.

BELOW *The Daimler Sovereign portfolio of posters and the cheaper brochure produced later.*

RIGHT and **BELOW**
Each Daimler poster was provided with brief comments. Poster No.1 was taken outside Ickworth House in Suffolk, emphasising 'the authority of the Daimler Sovereign' and comparing the house's regal facade to the Daimler grille. No.2 showed the interior of the car outside Syon Lodge in the south of England, emphasising the 'luxury' of the new model. No.3 depicted the car amidst the moors and mountains of Ross and Cromarty in Scotland to illustrate the car's 'strength'. And finally No.4 was taken in Blackfriars underpass in London and illustrated the words 'performance' and 'verve'.

LEFT *Four pieces of literature for two models in production for just a year: the V12-engined saloons of 1972. There is lack of consistency in the front cover treatment, and the Jaguar two-car 'beach' picture lacks any impact. The BL logo was now an integral part of the Jaguar name on the rear covers.*

CENTRE LEFT *BL photographers at this time seemed to have an obsession with logs, used in many pictures from E-types to this Jaguar (and Daimler) V12.*

BELOW *Rather uninspiring copy in the Daimler Double-Six material, with so much wasted space!*

V12s

Although the XJ bodyshell had always been designed to carry Jaguar's V12 engine, the Jaguar XJ12 wasn't launched until July 1972, the Daimler equivalent arriving a month later as the Double Six, reintroducing a name from the 1920s. Both cars had a limited lifespan, however, because in September 1973 the Series 2 versions were introduced. Despite this they benefited from individual promotional material.

For the Jaguar XJ12, whilst the size and format were very similar to the XJ6 offering, the material was by no means as exciting, which is a pity given the significance of what was the fastest production saloon car in the world at the time. Both a folder and a brochure were produced. Two cars featured on the front cover of the latter, set against a deserted beach, probably in North Wales since most of the inside shots used Portmerion (an Italianate village) as their backdrop. They don't show off the car to best advantage and the text is printed on unusual bright orange or mustard dyed paper!

The Daimler got a similar folder and brochure, though this time the same fluted radiator grille top and V12 insignia badge featured on both covers. Some of the internal pictures were obviously taken at the forestry location also used for a silver XJ12. The text on the opposite pages was arty, taking up little space on the stark white pages.

It is interesting here to reflect on the position of the Daimler marque, both within Jaguar and British Leyland. The standard of these brochures does not in any way compare to the first XJ6 brochure from 1968. The Daimler Double-Six brochure was printed by Waterloo and Sons, whereas the inferior Jaguar XJ12 equivalent was printed by Nuffield Press. The latter was then part of BL, and this heralded the start of the businesses coming together, with Nuffield printing material for Jaguar alongside that for models such as the Austin Allegro!

Long wheelbase versions of the XJs introduced in 1972 didn't warrant more than a simple black and white sheet for each brand. A real surprise, however, was that the launch of the most prestigious and expensive XJ of them all, the Daimler Double-Six Vanden Plas, was accompanied by no more than a mediocre 12in (305mm) square four-page folder!

The Daimler Double-Six Vanden Plas — long wheelbase.

XJ Series 2 models

From this point the whole issue of brochure material gets confusing, partly through the proliferation of models but also from the sheer number of brochures produced, most of which came from the Nuffield Press. Quality varied dramatically, and for some reason extraordinary quantities seem to have been printed of each. We need, therefore, to look at things slightly differently, as the Series 2 models represented the largest model segment and many brochures consequently took on the mantle of range material.

Taking an overview of the situation, new material was published for each year, grouping 1973/4, 1974/5, 1975/6, 1976/7, and 1978/9. For each model year there were both Jaguar and Daimler brochures, and in some cases numerous versions of them. This represents the most comprehensive coverage of a Jaguar model

range ever up to this point, with up to seven items for each year of production plus other material including leaflets, for a production run that lasted from 1973 to 1978. Quite a contrast to the 1968 to 1973 production run of the Series 1 cars.

The Series 2 offerings provide the best example so far of changing fashions, outlooks, and attitudes. For instance, the early issues are well produced on good quality paper, although with poor photographs, and are still published by Jaguar Cars with the BL logo discretely placed on the rear cover. However, the mid-term and later issues changed, progressively getting worse. As the paper stock deteriorated, so did the photographs, and the British Leyland UK Limited name and address and Leyland Cars insignia now appeared prominently, with no mention of Jaguar Cars. The layout and picture settings were in many cases a direct lift from the style used on contemporary family car material,

ABOVE *XJ Series 2, UK M-registered saloon and coupé brochures. These were normal landscape size and format and all, apart from two, featured wraparound cover designs.*

95

BELOW

The N-registered saloon and coupé material, featuring broad borders to the covers. There was additional, lesser material only for the coupés.

such as the Morris Marina – all confirming that Jaguar had lost their independence.

In contrast, the very last Series 2 material showed a distinct turnaround: better production, more lavish design, and a move away from the contemporary BL material. The name Jaguar even reappeared instead of British Leyland. This probably coincided with changes in management structure and the appointment of Jaguar man Bob Knight to the post of Managing Director. Jaguar was starting to re-establish its identity.

Launch material, produced in folder and brochure forms, showed different approaches for Jaguar and Daimler. For the former there

was a landscape wrap-around image for the covers – it's just a pity the effect was spoilt by electricity pylons in the background! The photographer also seems to have been obsessed with grass, as in many cases it obscures much of the cars. Text is conspicuous by its absence and the overall quality of production is poor.

The coupés at this time got equal coverage to the saloons, although in reality they didn't appear on the market until 1975, which lay beyond the life of these catalogues. Also a special Vanden Plas brochure was as significant as the other saloon version, despite the fact there was only one model, which sold in smaller numbers.

A new approach was tried for the N registration year material. There was a change to the front cover style, while the interior pages were all white text set against a coloured background, black for Daimler, brown for Jaguar. Brown was a very 'in' colour at the time! The Daimler brochure was much nicer, both in photography selection and content, although both were lacklustre compared to the benchmark Series 1 material.

For 1976/7 there were no less than five 16-page brochures plus a more basic 3.4-litre catalogue, at a time when Jaguar had truly lost their independence as confirmed by the Ryder Report in 1975. The Jaguar offering, for example, was definitely taking on the corporate identify of British Leyland, with the same style, design, and quality as all the other BL marques, regardless of their market position. The arty treatment to the front cover, of a minute car pictured on a muddy background, was worthless. Other pictures were clumsily taken studio affairs against dark backgrounds that did little for the Jaguar image.

Daimler models fared slightly better, with the car on the front cover set against a law court, but the other studio work came from the same source as the Jaguar shots. With the Coupé models supposedly in full-scale production they benefited from unique colour brochures of their own at this stage.

ABOVE and **NEXT PAGE** *1975 P-registered cars. Another revised range of material, but now produced on much thinner paper stock. All were reprinted for the following year with relevant pictures retouched to give them the replacement R registration letter.*

Some ingenuity was applied in the change of approach between the Daimler and Jaguar Coupé brochures, in their front covers for example. For Jaguar, the marketing department considered the car more applicable to a younger, more vibrant owner, hence the white coupé in an office block environment with a smart younger businessman complete with period sideburns and longish hair. Inside, the same car featured again, somewhat out of the limelight with two couples dressed up for the evening. (The photographer lacked direction or was concentrating on a nicely framed picture without emphasis on the actual car!) The equivalent Daimler Coupé covers took a slightly more traditional approach, with a black car set against the marble Birmingham Chamber of Commence building and an older owner in sombre suit with short hair.

The coupé cars had an unusual and useful window arrangement that allowed all the side windows to wind down completely, effectively turning the car into a pillarless example. The cars looked attractive like this and it should have been a good selling feature, but no one thought about making it so in the brochures!

For the new 3.4-litre model – supposedly a fleet entry car at a lower price and specification – the brochure was thinner, with a plain white

cover, but inside the car was depicted on several occasions being unwrapped by a chauffeur. This was another example of ill-conceived promotion, because the cheap model was in many respects featured in a better way than the larger-engined, more expensive models!

The new portrait-style brochures adopted for 1978 were an improvement, in quality of materials used, presentation, and photography, although now without any reference to the coupé models, which had been deleted from the range.

With no cars at all on the covers, which were colour coded according to brand, good use was made of double-fold pages to reveal larger-scale images. Back came heritage, and although the Leyland logo featured the Jaguar and Daimler brand names were prominent again. These brochures represented a pleasant return to the quality expected from top-of-the-range Jaguar material.

The appropriate Vanden Plas brochure is particularly interesting in that it is as substantial as the others, and the front cover strapline is evocative: 'Daimler with Coachwork by Vanden Plas'. With plenty of interspersed photographs of hand-finishing work, it is also the first integrated brochure to feature the DS420 Limousine, in no less than ten pages. This is a car we will return to later.

ABOVE *Material for the S-registered XJ saloons (Coupé models had been dropped by this time) switched to portrait format, with plain covers that varied in colour according to brand.*

LEFT, BELOW RIGHT and **BOTTOM** *Compare the Allegro picture of a businessman about to leave for work to the blurred image of the Jaguars by the water. Both are taken from equivalent brochures of the same period.*

The JAGUAR Four-Door Saloon Car Range. XJ 3·4, 42 and 53

Allegro 2
1100/1300 Models

ALLEGRO

A promise renewed

For many, the advent of the Jaguar XJ range heralded a new era of superlative motoring. An incomparable blend of design, performance, engineering and safety which has become the very hallmark of practical luxury.

Most certainly, a Jaguar is for people who value excellence and style. For people who care about craftsmanship and painstaking attention to detail. A special car for special people.

The unwavering maintenance of Jaguar values is one of the stable factors in a fast changing world. A promise of refined excellence between Jaguar and its motoring public.

The fulfilment of that promise was widely acclaimed in the XJ and Series 2 range.

Now, we renew that promise in the latest four-door range. Three cars of unmistakable pedigree.

We have made some subtle changes, in design and engineering. Nothing too drastic, of course, because our saloon car range is well established as the most outstanding in its class. Change for its own sake has no place in the Jaguar philosophy.

Of one thing you may be certain. The latest XJ saloons will take their rightful place just a little ahead of their predecessors, as one of the safest, most desirable and best value for money ranges Jaguar have ever offered.

Allegro 2
1300 4 door super

economy motoring in the grand manner

Features

100

ABOVE *There was a return to older and traditional values as Jaguar started to take control of its destiny, so this Daimler brochure for 1978 incorporates information on the heritage of the marque.*

RIGHT CENTRE *First sighting of the Daimler Limousine in a saloon brochure published in 1978. High quality images and foldout pages were employed to good effect.*

RIGHT *This centre spread comes from European literature for the Series 2s. The photographer (perhaps one of the BL crowd!) seems to have lost the plot. Not only does the picnic look scruffy, but where is the actual car? – there it is, lost in the background!*

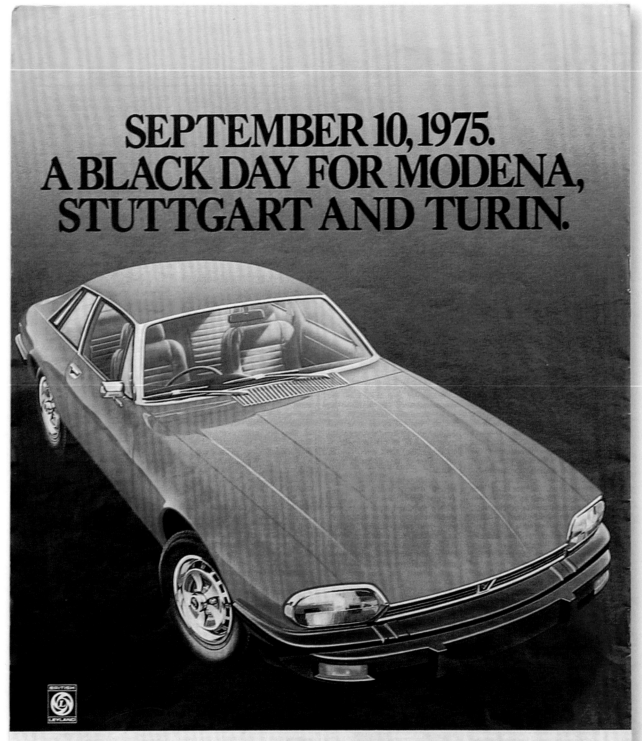

SEPTEMBER 10, 1975. A BLACK DAY FOR MODENA, STUTTGART AND TURIN.

What's good news for the British motor industry has to be bad news for our foreign competitors.

And the best news of this or any other year has to be the Jaguar XJS.

No other car made currently offers a comparable combination of performance and luxury at anywhere near the price.

Which explains why export orders for the XJS are already expected to be in excess of £20 million. In the first year.

Needless to say, performance of the XJS is startling. Zero to sixty takes under seven seconds. Top speed, where permissible, is in the region of 150 mph.

Yet this level of performance is achieved in levels of silence and safety that will astonish and delight you. As will the mpg figures.

Technically, the XJS has many features which are unique to Jaguar. And the list of luxury and safety features fitted as standard equipment is long and impressive.

Which is as it should be, considering that the XJS has been designed to be the definitive Jaguar.

Which makes it, in many ways, the definitive high-performance luxury car.

September 10, 1975. A great day for British motoring. And for Britain.

The Jaguar XJS
The car everyone dreams of.
But very, very few can ever own.

Printed by C. J. Mason & Sons Ltd., Bristol, BS13 7TP.

© IPC Transport Press.

XJ-S

The XJ-S was a new sporting model with which Jaguar hoped to capture a new market, so it deserved unique and special treatment in promotion.

The special launch brochure was a prestigious item, if unusual in many ways. It was almost 12in (305mm) square, a format only previously used for the folder of the Vanden Plas Series 1 saloon. The XJ-S offering came in a card slipcase that could also be (and was) used as a mailing envelope. This took the form of an old-style LP sleeve and had to be sealed using Sellotape – a very downmarket approach that showed a lack of detail planning.

The interior saw a return to onion-skin overlays (something not seen since the 1950s) which were used to feature the text. This apparently quality item suffered from the same misguided approach to design and photography experienced with other material at this time. It was probably conceived by the same people responsible for the 1976/7 XJ Series 2 brochure described above, since the dull front cover featured a minute red XJ-S on a winding road. Throughout the brochure only red cars were depicted, demonstrating limited imagination, even considering the small range of exterior colour schemes that were offered at launch.

The text featured an elongated romantic story that unfolded literally through the publication.

FAR LEFT The contemporary advertising campaign from Jaguar made optimistic claims as the company aimed the new XJ-S at a very different market to the E-type.

BELOW The XJ-S launch mailer was a mistake and the front cover of the brochure was odd, not doing enough to concentrate on the actual car.

ABOVE Reprints of the early XJ-S brochure involved changing the British registration suffix from N to S in a crude, amateurish way!

TOP This double-page spread seems to serve little purpose and is confusing to the eye.

Nowhere in this story was there any mention of the XJ-S, although the couple were obviously meant to be those depicted with the car.

Emphasising the international nature of the car, pictures focused on different countries and types of roads, and the car even changed registration numbers. Some pages were split into separate and disjointed boxed images, though others, with their pictures bleeding off all four edges, looked more impressive. This brochure was reprinted several times, at one point omitting the romantic story!

As the XJ-S was the most expensive production car from Jaguar at this time there was no need to produce cheaper, folder-style literature, but due to poor sales there were no updates to the first brochure other than those already mentioned.

The rest of the XJ-S story continues in the next chapter.

BELOW *A surprising contrast to the UK material can be seen in the equivalent US item which, although smaller, with less content, was actually very well designed and produced. A die-cut front emphasises the 'S'.*

BOTTOM *Excellent, well-lit studio photography, lots of detail images, and straightforward text about the car. This was certainly one of the best promotional items from the US up to this time.*

RIGHT *A perfect example from one of the British Leyland Group brochures. The still fairly new prestigious XJ6 is shown not only alongside a tank (in a bigger picture) but also adjacent to the lesser Triumph marque models. Over the page was the Morris range!*

BELOW *We can't leave the BL era without viewing the combined vehicle range booklets produced at this time. This is just a sample of them. Unfortunately they included Jaguar along with Austin Mini and every other car produced by the BL Group.*

BELOW *A selection of the many and varied brochures produced for the Daimler DS420 limousine.*

BOTTOM *Early promotional treatment for the limousine was very traditional indeed, as one would expect.*

The elegant and luxurious eight seater interior...

Never perhaps were spaciousness, comfort and luxurious appointments so thoughtfully planned as in this magnificent limousine. From the handsome fascia panel with its complete instrumentation to the expansive comfort of the rear seating, nothing has been spared to ensure the utmost enjoyment of the smooth and silent travel this Daimler provides.

Whether occupied by two persons or six, the spacious rear compartment affords generous accommodation in luxuriously furnished and comprehensively equipped surroundings. Lavish use is made of the finest quality materials—figured walnut cabinet work, deep nylon pile carpeting over thick felt underlay, distinctive West of England cloth or finest leather upholstery. A high-efficiency fresh air heating system is provided, controlled from a panel in the left-hand armrest. Separate controls are provided for the front compartment, which is also finished to an extremely high standard.

Complete details of all the interior fitments of this limousine will be found in the specification sheet enclosed with this brochure.

"The Daimler Limousine is here, Your Excellency."

Limousines

We should make mention here of the Daimler DS420 limousine, a specialist vehicle created within the BL Group but very much a part of Jaguar. Announced in 1968, it remained in production until 1992 and featured heavily in promotional material. Although its existence spanned several decades, the relevant details are all given here.

RIGHT *Later material followed the in-house style of brochure design. This example features the country house backdrop to good effect…*

BELOW *…but also, unusually, includes an example of the limousine with Dralon upholstery!*

BELOW *A bit of ingenuity is used in this brochure.*

EXCLUSIVE, INSIDE AND OUT

EXCLUSIVE, INSIDE AND OUT

LEFT *These examples show a dramatic contrast in the type of person who would use a limousine, c1970s into the 1980s – from the well-endowed Lord and Lady who might well attend a Queen's ball…*

LEFT *…to the high-powered business executive requiring chauffeur transport…*

LEFT *...the newly-rich couple on their way to the races...*

LEFT *...and the visiting tourists in a hired car!*

4.0 litre Convertible

The Legend Grows

Vanden Plas

JAGUAR
XJ-S XJ-SC
3.6
V12

JAGUAR XJ-S

JAGUAR
Daimler

This publication described the general features of the Jaguar XJ-S range. However, specifications and availability do vary from country to country the separate specification sheets for specific details of the cars available in any particular country.

XJ·S 3.6 COUPE

XJ-SC 3·6 CABRIOLET | XJ-S 3·6 COUPE

A return to quality

The British Leyland era was followed by a period of transition from public to private ownership. A new man, John Egan, was at the helm, a new high-tech saloon, the XJ40, was launched, and a new air of individualism and confidence was evident at Jaguar. Quality improved, as did sales. A new slogan was introduced for the company's advertising – 'The Legend Grows' – and prominent use was made of the leaper motif. This was also an interesting era of change and uncertainty, because different approaches were again tried in marketing.

BELOW *An intriguing
Series 3 brochure
picture photographed
against a backdrop of a
power station, perhaps
emphasising the power
behind Jaguar! For
some reason Jaguar
produced a hardcover
version of this brochure.*

The same style of large-sized launch brochure (with mailer) deemed necessary for the XJ-S was utilised for the new XJ saloon. This was conventional in design, however, with traditional vehicle finishing clearly in evidence. Pictures were well composed in a variety of industrial and dramatic backdrops, and at the rear a pocket held three full-sized, full-colour photographs, each depicting a different model.

The Daimler variants continued to be treated separately, at least until 1985. The early 1979 literature was smaller, but no less prestigious and different, and was understated. A simple white portfolio opened to reveal a Daimler fluted radiator grille and badge on the front cover of the brochure. Inside it was traditionally laid out, with all the then current Daimlers covered, including the Vanden Plas and the Limousine. Images echoed Daimler's typical customers, with cars set against country houses, with chauffeurs. The photographers and copywriters showed good initiative too, a good example of this being the double-page spread

that opened out to show the dashboard in all its glorious detail, no less than 2ft (0.6m) wide!

By 1981 John Egan was already making a difference to quality and image. One of the first major tangible changes came with the introduction of the high efficiency (HE) version of the V12 engine, providing improved fuel economy. With better build quality, all models were improved.

Due to its poor sales there wasn't the money to produce further unique XJ-S brochures, so for two years the sports model shared publicity material with the more profitable and faster-selling XJ saloons.

With improvements in engine efficiency and build quality, and the return of a little traditionalism in the form of wood veneer and exterior chrome, the XJ-S improved dramatically, further helped by a return to racing via the back door with the Tom Walkinshaw racing team (TWR) in the European Touring Car Championship. The XJ saloons benefited similarly.

BELOW *A quality image and good use of a double-spread for the Daimler Series 3 launch brochure.*

BELOW *The first two pages inside the 1981 brochure opened out into a four-page spread, for which the photographer had used graduated filtering to good effect.*

For 1981 the new portrait format Jaguar brochure featured both models. This was a quality item that made excellent use of double- and in some cases four-page spreads.

Daimler was still earning its right to a separate offering, with red becoming the recognised colour for the marque (green, of course, was for Jaguar). Even more effort was put into this brochure, with individually produced imagery by well known professional artists, 'snappers' Lord Lichfield (who himself owned a Daimler) and David Bailey.

An interesting turnaround in the mid-1980s saw a fall-off of interest in the Daimler marque

and the rise to prominence of the Jaguar XJ, with a new, more upmarket model stealing the Sovereign name.

The first brochure now exuded a new, stronger emphasis on the quality of the Jaguar marque, its products, and its pedigree, with no less than two pages of Jaguar history and two more on its racing heritage. On the following page was a distinct link of the old with the new, with the words 'technology' and – a return to another era – 'pace and grace' (they didn't go so far as to say 'space'!). With lots of thoughtful quality photographs of the cars this was a well-produced brochure, deserving of the new era for Jaguar.

The equivalent Daimler offering took on the same style, even down to the green covers. The range of models was now reduced to just three, including the Limousine, and one of the interesting aspects of this brochure is that the latter is featured in a rare two-tone blue paintwork and with Velour trim!

In 1986 Jaguar felt it was time for a mammoth range book with no less than 52 pages, issued just prior to the demise of the six-cylinder XJ models and before the debut of the new XJ40 saloons. It covered all the cars, including the XJ-S and Daimlers, with a gold leaper prominently

displayed on the front cover. As if to emphasise Jaguar's newfound status, John Egan himself provided an introduction, and there were no less than 12 pages devoted to the history and development of the cars. Each model was then covered in turn, with new photography.

V12s stand alone

The launch of the new XJ40 in 1986 meant that only the XJ12 and Double-Six Series 3 models continued in production, albeit limited, for an amazing six years.

BELOW LEFT *A new air of confidence for the marque from the mid-1980s – an emphasis on green and gold, and concentration on heritage and quality.*

BELOW *'Individually signed masterpieces' is a good strapline for any car brochure!*

BOTTOM *The heritage of the marque came to the fore again in the John Egan era.*

FAR RIGHT TOP *An incredible selection of XJ-S material from 1982 through to 1988 in two distinct styles. Also included here are the Canadian and US equivalents.*

FAR RIGHT BELOW *The new Cabriolet received excellent coverage in the post-1983 brochures, despite the fact that it was initially not exported to the USA, was only available with the smaller engine, and was promoted as a special-order model.*

In 1987, with the publicity machine geared up for the XJ40, the Series 3 offering wasn't particularly strong. Following the same design style as for the new car, there were just six pages on both the Jaguar XJ12 and the Daimler Double-Six.

The following year Jaguar rethought the promotional aspects of the V12s and created a more extensive 16-page brochure in the same style but with the addition of headlight detail on the cover to good effect. Despite the expected low production levels of these models an entirely new set of pictures was commissioned. Initial photographs featured the two cars set against the background of Gleneagles in Scotland, followed by a range of interesting

backdrops from a German autobahn to Number 10 Downing Street in London. A couple of pages were devoted to the craftsmanship behind the car, not least a picture of a radiator grille being made, something normally reserved for the likes of Rolls-Royce!

XJ-S model expansion

Returning to the ongoing fortunes of the XJ-S, which had enjoyed a remarkable turnaround in sales and image, Jaguar now had the confidence to promote the car separately and use it as a launch-pad for a new six-cylinder engine appearing in both Coupé and Cabriolet models.

TOP RIGHT *Pages from the very last unique Series 3 V12 brochure produced in 1988: new photography and great emphasis on craftsmanship.*

RIGHT *Downing Street in London was chosen to photograph the luxurious Daimler Double-Six – but of course, the Prime Minister did have one of these cars.*

FAR RIGHT and
BELOW *Superior
production and unique
artwork epitomise XJ-S
promotional material of
the late 1980s and early
1990s, the best Jaguar
had produced for this
model up to that time.*

Despite the Cabriolet only remaining in production for four years, Jaguar's new confidence and improving financial position prompted the production of no less than four brochures covering this model, although incorporating the other variants as well.

XJ-S brochures become more lavish starting with the 1988 launch of the Convertible model. It represented a major investment for Jaguar and was the flagship of the range, being the most expensive sporting model they had ever produced.

Inside the 1988 brochure the racing pedigree was now strongly emphasised and all-new modernistic images were published, putting the car firmly into a different dimension.

This brochure covered all the XJ-S models, not being limited to the very expensive Convertible, although the latter did have 12 pages to itself.

For 1993 there was yet another and more lavish brochure, this time in the form of a green portfolio, something of a return to the best of pre-war Jaguar material. There was also a green folder this time, virtually a copy of the type used for the XJ40 saloon (see later), which contained a 12-page booklet on the history of the marque and a 36-page booklet on the XJ-S. The images used were taken from the 1991 issue, reprinted in 1992, although by now Jaguar had introduced the 4.0-litre Convertible, which was also featured.

RIGHT *The corporate
confidence came
through from 1988,
even on the front cover
with the understated
metallic silver-outlined
leaper and just the
letters 'XJ-S'.*

4.0 litre Convertible

ABOVE *Following the 1991 facelift of the XJ-S, the same style of brochure was used but with all-new images. Shot in Bermuda, Jaguar emphasised that the XJ-S had finally achieved its original aim of catering for the luxury-lifestyle market previously the domain of cars like the Mercedes SL.*

Later that year another new brochure had to be produced because of trim changes. The images used inside were all studio produced. Yet another printing took place in 1994, with more pages and a different (white) cover. This flurry of material was obviously to capitalise on the revised specifications and to push sales in view of the forthcoming planned launch of an entirely new car in 1996.

At the end of the year yet another new XJ-S brochure appeared, produced to cover the Celebration models (the final edition), although it doesn't actually call them that. A new corporate style, devised for the then new X-300 saloons (see next chapter), was adopted for this very last XJ-S material, the cover being white with an enhanced three-quarter frontal view of a red car with the text angled around the bonnet.

That's not the end of the XJ-S story however. We should also take a look at what was happening abroad, where some superb brochures were produced, predominantly for US consumption. Though there are too many to

cover in detail, the photographs give some idea of the type of material published.

And lastly there has been quite a proliferation of material produced for the XJR-S models, the low volume cars which later formed part of the JaguarSport operation jointly run by Jaguar and TWR. The factory sanctioned and later produced material specifically for these cars and it is surprising to look back at how much was published. Although never over-the-top in quality terms, the volume of material produced must have been designed to push the brand forward in marketing terms, though sales didn't necessarily follow!

XJ40

In 1986 Jaguar launched their new XJ6 models (commonly known as XJ40 after their development name). Virtually entirely new and desperately awaited, marketing was vital not only to encourage existing customers to buy Jaguar again but also to cultivate entirely new

RIGHT and **BELOW**
*1992 to 1994 XJ-S
material blossomed,
with new artwork,
images, and copy plus
a variety of different
cover styles.*

RIGHT *Last-of-the-line XJ-S brochure with very different cover treatment used for the new saloon models.*

BELOW CENTRE and **BOTTOM** *Clever use of a centre spread to show the hood up and down in the final Celebration brochure.*

LEFT *Three examples of US LP-sized quality brochures on the XJ-S from the mid-1980s. Strong, simple front cover images, excellent photography inside, coverage given to the Group 44 Jaguar racing team, and all printed on excellent quality paper.*

LEFT *Heritage repeats itself consistently in the US material, but mostly in specifically produced images which incorporated the new cars. Some of the US photography by this stage was superb, with excellent lighting treatment and great backdrops – just what a prospective XJ-S owner wanted to see and aspire to.*

LEFT *A choice move to lifestyle photography – why wouldn't the owner of this XJ-S also own the boat?*

BELOW *The US material at this time also promoted the unique Hess & Eissenhardt Convertibles, produced to special order in the States for a while.*

FROM A STORIED TRADITION OF OPEN MOTORCARS COMES ONE OF THE MOST EXCITING V-12 JAGUARS EVER BUILT: THE XJ-S CONVERTIBLE BY HESS & EISENHARDT.

More than half a century ago, the Jaguar name first appeared on a sleek and stylish open motorcar: the legendary SS Jaguar 100. That remarkable automobile inspired a series of convertibles that would forever link the pleasures of open-air motoring to the Jaguar marque.

Now, the classic open Jaguar is reborn.

A worthy successor to open Jaguars of the past, this beautiful soft top conversion is skillfully executed by Hess & Eisenhardt, a custom coachbuilder of great renown since 1876. A vivid performer, the XJ-S convertible utilizes the same advanced mechanical systems as the XJ-S grand touring coupe. These include Jaguar's powerful V-12 engine, fully independent suspension and precise rack and pinion steering.

Within the convertible's spacious cabin, the driver enjoys uncommonly luxurious appointments. Fragrant, hand-selected leather covers the comfortable yet supportive seats. Polished natural wood veneers grace the dashboard and door panels. A most elegant machine, the XJ-S convertible provides the perfect ambience for open-air motoring. It is available by special order through your Jaguar dealer.

THE XJS CONVERTIBLE

Advancing the Art of Grand Touring

The Jaguar XJ-S Coupe

LEFT *What an excellent choice from the US photographer. The car sits well against its backdrop, the colours are co-ordinated, and the image is highly detailed and well lit.*

BELOW *There are lots of instances of pictures specially commissioned for US promotional material that incorporate classic Jaguars as well.*

127

BELOW *There was an amazing amount of material for the XJR-S models, from single sheets to a large-scale brochure, despite the low production numbers.*

markets by stealing business from the established and successful competition – BMW, Mercedes, and soon Lexus.

It is fair to say that nearly all the material produced for this model was of a very good quality. The commonly used white covered, square format brochure was chosen for the launch material. Interestingly despite the 'newness' of the XJ40, the cover remained plain. Inside, however, the first three pages spread out into a fabulous studio image of the Daimler version. The next ten pages were devoted to the development and technology behind the new car, with a further two pages on the traditional touches of wood and leather craftsmanship. This was a substantial item of 40 pages plus folders

on prices, specifications, and colours/trim. A new version was published in 1988 with slightly revised cover treatment and a completely new set of photographs.

In contrast the US launch brochure created more impact, the front cover taking the 'Evolution of the Species' (cat in jungle) theme. As the launch over there was later than in the UK, the opportunity was taken to publish magazine comment cuttings at the beginning. This was followed by a striking three-page colour spread of a maroon car in the jungle.

Ten pages were again devoted to the technological aspects of the car, most of which were different to the UK equivalent. Apart from some more copy at the rear on the model's

LEFT *A special edition XJ-S was the Le Mans, produced to commemorate their win in the 24-hour race. A simple card folder was issued to promote it.*

BELOW *From a US brochure, the Collection Rouge model got more than adequate promotion.*

BELOW *From one of the last and most lavish of US brochures, this red XJ-S is depicted in a garden-party environment – so much better than the BL-era XJ Coupé example depicted in the previous chapter!*

BELOW *Superbly produced studio imagery for the 1994 US brochure. The US only got the best, most well-equipped models.*

BOTOM *An interesting package, sent out via the dealers, to encourage people to buy the last-of-the-line Celebration XJ-S*

models, with a certificate and promise to buy the car back 12 months later in exchange for the new XK8.

LEFT *Taken from the first XJ40 brochure, this image was commonly used during the car's early life. The same treatment was later used to promote the X-300 models.*

CENTRE *Great emphasis was put on the technical aspects of the new car. It was the first time, for example, that split-away drawings like this were used.*

BELOW *Another first for the XJ40 material was the introduction of quite complex photography, in this instance making use of multi-images to create the car with its roof 'removed'.*

JAGUAR VANDEN PLAS:
THE COACHMAKER'S ART

EVOLUTION OF THE SPECIES

...atti.
of the
rns the
...ailable,
...to
...he

simply luxurious. In addition to
unique, distinguishing exterior em-
bellishments, this remarkable automobile offers a sensually luxurious
passenger compartment, reminiscent of those found in the elegant

carriages once constructed for European royalty. The Vanden Plas cabin
features heated front seats, stitched
leather upholstery, a contoured rear
seat with headrests, extensive use
of burl walnut trim, rear seat burl

walnut picnic tables, rear seat overhead reading lamps, and fleece-like
footwell rugs. Special Vanden Plas
mechanical equipment includes
heated headlight washers and a limited slip differential.

TOP LEFT *The jungle theme for the US launch of the XJ40.*

TOP MAIN *One of the many quality spreads from the US brochure that make this a particularly pleasing publication.*

traditional features, the rest was made up entirely of double-page colour spreads, creating a high quality look for this publication.

3s and 40s integration

For 1989 there was another new approach with the amalgamation of the XJ40 and Series 3 models into an enormous 12in x 12in (305mm x 305mm) 50-page quality booklet. The first 40 pages were devoted to the XJ40 range with superbly executed photographs, arguably the best produced up to that time. The Series 3 cars got 16 pages, which was perhaps disproportionate in comparison to the sales achieved. All the images were new, many being of a surreal nature. Text was minimal and at the back there was a separate six-page

specification booklet on all the models.

This brochure was reprinted for 1990 with front cover amendments. This was perhaps merely to help differentiate between the two brochures, as the later one covered the then new 4.0-litre-engined cars. Now of 56 pages, the majority of the content was a carryover, although the photographs of V12 models were new and they got an extra two pages of coverage.

Separating Jaguar and Daimler

From 1991 the company separated the two marques again for the first time since 1985. In hindsight this was probably done in readiness for the 1993 launch of the V12-engined XJ40 saloons, but for the year in question the material

XJ6 SOVEREIGN DAIMLER

DAIMLER DOUBLE SIX

only showed the old Series 3 models.

Both the Jaguar and Daimler issues had similar front cover treatment. Still of the same large 12in (305mm) size with predominately white facing, each had an enclosed central box area, green for the Jaguar and plum for the Daimler. The Jaguar item had 36 pages, the Daimler 28. The V12 had ten pages of coverage in the Jaguar brochure with some superb photography from various locations. Not seen for many years, a small artist's impression of the car also appeared on one page.

For the Daimler brochure heritage prevailed, and both models were again posed together in some instances. Surprisingly both had equal coverage, with some excellent images reflecting the Daimler's 'prestige', with the cars backdropped against the Houses of

Parliament, Sotheby's auction house, and a country estate.

XJ40 stands alone

In 1993 Jaguar introduced the V12 (6.0 litre) variants of the XJ40. For the launch material Jaguar and Daimler were treated separately, but both followed the same format of a portfolio folder in coloured card (green for Jaguar, maroon for Daimler). Both were embossed with hot gold foil stamping depicting the brands. This type of folder was also made available for the XJ-S, but in that instance it carried the insignia on the cover.

Within the folder a brief history booklet was accompanied by individual model brochures – one each for the XJ6, Sovereign,

TOP *Some interesting photography from the mid-term saloon material, trying to promote the cars to a wider, younger, more contemporary audience.*

ABOVE *Even the very traditional Daimler Double-Six received the same contemporary approach to imagery.*

FAR RIGHT *Examples of the portfolio style of material produced later for the XJ saloon models.*

FAR RIGHT BELOW *Taken from the 1991 brochure, this picture epitomises a sense of security and a return to traditional values in response to a fall-off in car sales. The landowner with his green wellies might well be a Jaguar owner of the time.*

and XJ12 in the case of Jaguar, while the Daimler folder just featured the 4.0-litre and Double-Six.

The final XJ40 brochures were published for the 1994 model year. These comprised 50 pages for the Jaguar and 18 for the Daimler, both in 10½in x 12in (267mm x 305mm) format, and featured simple white varnished covers with ghosted images of the radiator grilles. Inside were mostly new pictures and revised text according to changes in model specification. These were excellent publications in their own right, if not up to the standard of some of the earlier work on this model.

XJ40 model specifics

In 1993 Jaguar introduced the 3.2-litre S model, a supposedly sporty version of the XJ40, to entice a younger market. It had its own literature in the form of a simple portrait style four-page colour folder. The grey cover with a large 'S' featured a maroon car, while the inside folded out to reveal a red car across the centre spread. A 4.0-litre version was also offered but this didn't get the benefit of a unique folder.

In 1994 there was also the Gold model, effectively a limited edition end-of-line model with a 3.2-litre engine and styling and trim

Daimler Double Six   Daimler 4.0 litri

RIGHT TOP *A good comparison picture of the 'old brigade' Series 3 alongside the 'new kid on the block' XJ40 – one of the few times that both models were featured together for such close examination.*

RIGHT BOTTOM *This gentleman craftsman working on the boxwood inlay of a Daimler's trim panel was well known, as he appeared in Jaguar and Daimler brochures many times over the years.*

Costante ricerca della qualità

Sovereign

RIGHT *A selection of the folders produced for selected low-production XJ40 models: the 3.2-litre S and Gold, and the Majestic long wheelbase.*

BELOW *One low-production model that didn't get its own folder was the 4.0-litre S model, which was included within a later XJ40 brochure.*

Combining all the best specially tailor-made features carefully into a coherent package, the new XJ6 3.2S and XJ6 4.0S models possess their own very individual character - strikingly sporting, yet still with that unmistakable Jaguar style.

Externally, this special character is immediately apparent. The colour-keyed radiator grille vanes and door mirrors together with the silver Jaguar badge of a cat's head and fitted foglamps, indicate that these are cars for the motorist who enjoys spirited driving. This impression is confirmed by the sporty 7 x 16 in. 5-spoke alloy wheels, which have cat's head badges against a ruby-finish background. Further distinction is provided by single upper and double lower side stripes, plus a 3.2S or 4.0S badge below the side indicator repeater lamp, matching the ruby wheel badges; matt black window surrounds also contribute to the sleek exterior style.

The rear of the cars, with minimum chrome and with a stylish colour-keyed infill panel surrounding the number plate, is discreetly badged just '3.2S' or '4.0S'. The rear lamps are either dark grey or red, depending on which of the optional paint colours is chosen. Four metallic finishes and two solid paint colours are available. The alloy road wheels and side stripes are finished in either eggshell or silver, as appropriate to the chosen paint colour.

To match the character of the XJ6 3.2S and XJ6 4.0S, the suspension system has been modified and developed to give tauter and extremely agile handling, without loss of ride comfort. Included in this special system are up-rated dampers and a new stiffer anti-roll bar.

RIGHT *Insignia folder that gave details of unique exterior and interior colour schemes and other bespoke enhancements to standard production models.*

BELOW *Looking like it could, rather than actually supplying extra performance, the XJR saloons were always featured separately in their own promotional material.*

BELOW *Typically English settings to promote English automobiles in US brochures. The Vanden Plas remains to this day a model type specifically geared to the American market, representing the top-of-the-range saloon model.*

enhancements. Again a four-page folder was produced, this time in landscape format with a gold cover supposed to look like a gold ingot.

Other special XJ40 editions included a full-colour folder for the very rare Majestic long wheelbase model (of which only 50 were manufactured). There was also the Insignia folder covering bespoke finishes to production models (which covered the XJS as well). Though only around 200 of these cars were actually made, in varying degrees of trim enhancement, this is another of those folders which seems to have been printed in large quantities despite the fact that the cars were expensive and very few were produced.

Lastly there was the XJR model, which started out as a special limited edition from TWR (who also produced the XJ-S equivalent mentioned earlier). Initially they hand-finished the cars, but later they were assembled completely in-house at Jaguar. Several folders were produced, from the original 3.6-litre up to the last 4.0-litre models.

Other range brochures

By necessity we have had to amalgamate the coverage of models like the XJ and XJ-S, but there were also other offerings available during this period. For example, numerous fold-out

BELOW Typically English settings to promote English automobiles in US brochures. The Vanden Plas remains to this day a model type specifically geared to the American market, representing the top-of-the-range saloon model.

leaflets were produced, similar to those for the XJ and E-type mentioned in the previous chapter. A good example of these came out in 1983/4 with the new 'green' emphasis. On the cover three pictures covered the XJ, Daimler, and XJ-S. This one opened out into an A3 poster size, double-sided, with some nicely contrived settings for the cars, but very little copy except for an A5 area set aside merely to give fuel consumption figures at various speeds. This type of material was usually given away at events and shows and at casual introductions at the dealerships.

In the US special brochures and literature were prepared at two levels: the simple leaflet and a more complex brochure. One such interesting item is a small 7in (178mm) square full-colour booklet with a reflected leaper on the cover. Naturally the cars used for the photography were US-specced models, but the majority were photographed in the UK at typically British locations like a mock-Tudor residence, a cobbled courtyard in a country village, and outside the London International Stamp Centre.

This is an interesting brochure for another reason, because on the plain black back cover the following information reveals how the US market perceived the cars and the company at this time – remember this was 1986, during the privatisation era of Jaguar, at a time when quality was improving:

'The Legend Grows.

'Today's Jaguar motor cars are the evolutionary product of gradual refinement. Built by dedicated workers who are also

ABOVE *We can't leave this period without mentioning the low volume production supercar Jaguar created in the XJ220. Despite being the most expensive production car they had ever produced, and despite all the publicity they put behind it, the actual promotional material – comprising a large-format colour brochure accompanied by lesser ephemera – was a little disappointing.*

company stockholders, they are the most reliable Jaguars ever offered…'

The final words on this cover read 'ENJOY TOMORROW, BUCKLE UP TODAY', perhaps an obligatory Federal statement to promote the use of seat belts.

Range leaflets expanded (literally) in the UK, opening out to double sided A2 and A3 sizes in colour. With emphasis on the cover given to

'The Legend Grows' and the leaper motif, such material featured large single poster images on one side and detailed pictures of all the then current models, plus racing and classic heritage.

In conclusion this was an exciting period for Jaguar, leading up to 1988 when they sold more cars than in any previous year in the company's history. Now things were hotting up, with a new owner imminent.

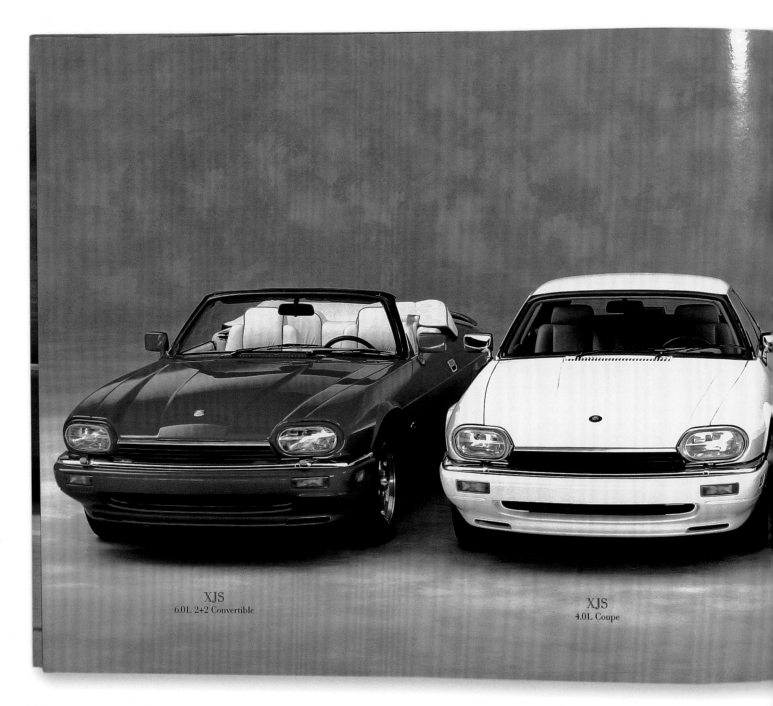

XJS
6.0L 2+2 Convertible

XJS
4.0L Coupe

BELOW *Later US material featuring the saloons and XJSs in 1993*

XJ6
4.0L Sedan

XJ12
6.0L Sedan

Into Ford ownership

This period in Jaguar's history starts in 1994 with the final demise of the XJ40 and the introduction of the first new saloon built with Ford money, the X-300, the first of a new range of cars with a strong relationship to Jaguar's heritage and, to a certain degree, retro styling.

BELOW *The front cover of the New XJ Series launch brochure depicted these three stacked radiator grilles, which became a feature of the material produced for these models.*

FAR RIGHT TOP *An unusual feature of the X-300 launch brochure was this onion-skin with styling drawings, making a very attractive presentation. Another similar page depicted the engine and allied features.*

The X-300 was marketed as 'The New XJ Series', reviving the 'series' title from the old days. Another revived 'pitch' involved more prestigious launch material (even a return to onion-skins). Even greater emphasis was put on quality, from photographs to copy, to the paper stock used. Finally, there was a trend towards more regular updating of the brochures and the provision of separate material for individual models.

The corporate look to promotional material was even more evident from here on in, but even so there was also a degree of 'trial and error' in some designs.

X-300 saloons

The New Series saloons were launched in September 1994, the emphasis being on the retro styling, AJ16 multi-coil engines (including

the first production supercharged model), and the other technological advancements that enabled a range of different models with the same bodyshell to satisfy very different markets. This became a key ploy in the marketing material, emphasising the various advantages of each model.

The launch brochure was a very prestigious affair and is certainly one of the key pieces of material produced post-war. Though a mere 26 pages for the introductory brochure on the background to the model range, it was accompanied by a wealth of other information and a mailer envelope, this time (unlike that for the XJ-S) well made and post-friendly!

The main thrust of other X-300 material for the first year of production centred around three model brochures, all in the same style and format. These split the models into three

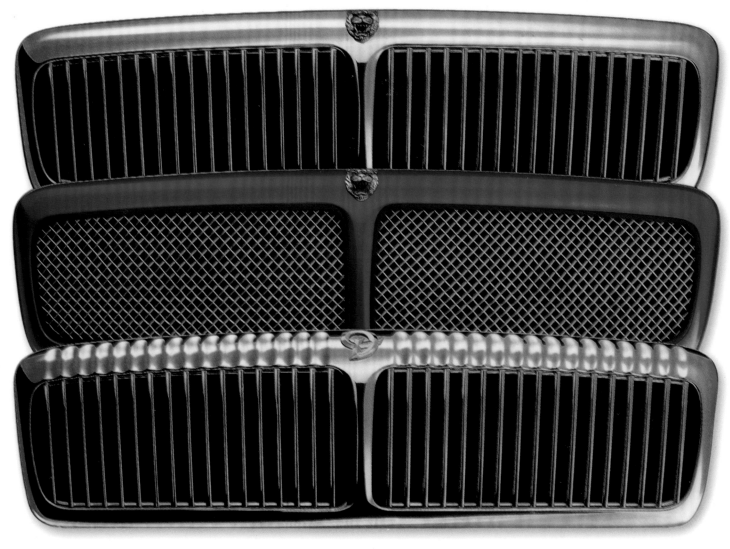

BELOW *The impressive and comprehensive launch material provided for the X-300 models in 1994 consisted of a brochure on the development of the models, a colour and trim guide, a complete price booklet, a compact 16-page booklet on the AJ16 engines, and a 32-page booklet on the whole range (including the 1994 XJ-S models).*

ABOVE *The post-launch brochures were split into model categories, with front cover treatment first seen on the very last version of the XJ-S material discussed earlier.*

categories – traditional Jaguar (XJ6, Sovereign, and XJ12), Sports (Sport and XJR), and Daimler (Six and Double Six).

With an excellent layout and superbly produced digitally enhanced pictures, including full interior images and moody dashboard layouts, these were a very effective way of promoting the cars. In contrast to the square look of the XJ40, much emphasis was placed on the curvaceous nature of the X-300, some of the script even being wrapped around the curves of the bodywork.

For 1996 the brochures were reprinted with more pages and revised cover designs, but with the same radiator grille treatment. They now covered the new long wheelbase models, and there were a lot of new images, making them

quite expensive to produce. But the cars were selling well.

Slightly later in 1996 Jaguar issued a separate smaller seven-page card folder specifically on the long wheelbase Jaguar models. There seems little explanation for this folder, as the date on it indicates that it was released after the launch of the previous brochures which already included the long wheelbase cars.

The Century

To celebrate the centenary of the Daimler marque in 1996 a limited edition Daimler Century model was announced. Equipped with every conceivable extra and available with either six- or twelve-cylinder engines, it deserved a

Jaguar XJ6.

Exceptional performance and unique presence.

Daimler Six & Daimler Double Six
Gleaming coachwork and the unmistakable aroma of rich leather.

XJ Sport & XJR Supercharged
A Sporting Heritage second to none.

XJ6, XJ Executive & Sovereign
Unmistakably classic lines.

ABOVE *A good example of photography promoting the curves of the new bodywork – note the almost subliminal reference to them achieved by posing the car against the arches of the viaduct.*

LEFT *The revised X-300 brochure style for 1997.*

ABOVE *An interesting comparison between one of the X-300 brochures and that featuring the Daimler DS420 limousine, showing how many pictures were altered digitally to save the cost of reshooting.*

special folder, akin to the old Vanden Plas Series 1 idea but much better executed. With gold hot foil stamping everywhere and parchment half-pages inside covering the history of the marque and this particular model, and a list of the extensive standard equipment, it is a very nice item – albeit somewhat superfluous in view of the fact that only 200 cars were produced and they all sold within the first few weeks!

The Executive

The 'Executive' badge had been used before by Jaguar, particularly for some overseas markets in the Series 2 XJ period, and the name was resurrected for a new X-300 model in 1997. Its card four-page launch folder was produced with a green cover and a sepia photograph of a male executive reading accompanied by a female colleague.

The name was a deliberate choice, as Jaguar explained within the text of the brochure: 'The Jaguar XJ Executive is a highly focused vehicle. Its very name confirms a commitment to a specific kind of Jaguar owner…'. With enhanced specification as a cross-breed between the standard XJ6 and the Sport models, it filled a gap in the range and was an attempt to capture a younger market for the marque. However, because the brochure took much of its style and content from other Jaguar material it didn't seem to fit the type of owner the car was aimed at.

Despite the short lifespan of the X-300 saloons, yet another set of brochures was published in 1997, the last year of production. Of square format and introducing a corporate style in keeping with the XK8 brochures of the time, there were again three distinct issues, of which the XJ6 version now included the Executive but not the XJ12 (which had been deleted from the range in April). Most of the interior was merely revamped from previous issues.

LEFT and **BELOW**
The luxury and style of the limited edition Century models was well represented in this special folder produced in 1996.

RIGHT *The new style of X-300 material for 1997, the last year of production.*

BELOW *A later example of the superb photography produced for the X-300 brochures. The bridge emphasises the long low look of the car.*

XJ6, XJ Executive & Sovereign
Unmistakably classic lines.

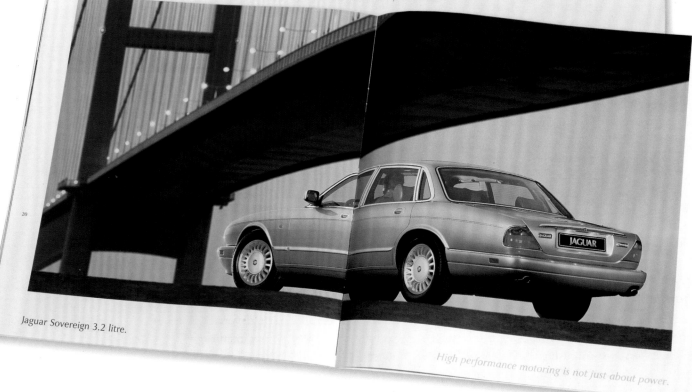

20

Jaguar Sovereign 3.2 litre.

21

High performance motoring is not just about power.

For overseas markets various X-300 brochures were produced, some in different formats to the normal style. Good design and ingenuity were evident even if most of the pictures were not of as high a quality as in the UK offering, despite the fact that the US market was so important to Jaguar. But this same criticism applies to most US material discussed so far.

XJ8

The XJ8 models that superseded the X-300 in 1997 and ran through to 2002 provide a very interesting comparison in the way they were marketed. The XJ8 was a natural progression from its predecessor, using the X-300 body style mated to the new AJ-V8 engine that had first appeared in the XK8 in 1996.

Initial brochure material followed the same square format and was produced to the by now usual high standard, the major difference being the amalgamation of models into just two categories (and thus two brochures), Jaguar and Daimler.

A new style of plainer front cover with scripted 'V8 XJ series' emblem was adopted. Major emphasis was played on the technical aspects, particularly – and naturally – on the V8 engine, with cutaways and lots of new images of detail and development work. Excellent full-colour double-page spread images of each model introduced the four pages devoted to each car, along with studio-produced pictures and good, interesting text. Because the interiors were new, they got greater coverage than in the X-300 material. The Daimler version placed greater

BELOW *The US X-300 models differed in external appearance, with a different boot pressing. Note the Vanden Plas name still used on the top-of-the-range models.*

FAR RIGHT TOP *Inside the 'veneered' US brochure can be found excellent and innovative promotional images. Here a dramatic close-up of the X-300 front is* *contrasted to an onion-skin print of a 2.4 saloon from the mid-1950s.*

FAR RIGHT BELOW *From the same 1996 US brochure, this spread emphasises the heritage and classic model background of the brand. Numerous pictures cover older cars* *from E-type to S-type. The strapline here is a little difficult to comprehend – 'The Rulers of the Road Drive Softly and Carry a V12'!*

JAGUAR

Specifications and colours are subject to change.
Jaguar Canada, Inc., Bramalea, Ontario, Canada. Printed in Canada 40M 10/95

THE RULERS OF THE ROAD
DRIVE SOFTLY AND CARRY A V12.

ABOVE *Examples of the different styles of brochure used for the XJ8 models from 1997 to 2002.*

emphasis on the tradition and quality aspects of the cars.

Both these launch publications were exceptionally well produced and were ideal marketing tools. They set the style for several years, not only for saloons but for XK sports cars as well.

In 1999 both brochures were revamped with new covers and different images. Though at first glance they looked the same, there were actually subtle differences to the car interior pictures, necessary because of modifications to the trim.

For 2000 there were two more catalogues, the

same format for the Jaguar but with a more striking cover depicting just part of an XJ8 front. The tone of this brochure changed to one of 'discovering the magic' and 'in touch with control', each phrase accompanying stunning studio images.

The Daimler item is interesting in its own right because it adopted a different format, although of the same size. It was hardbound with a cream textured cover and the Daimler name embossed in gold foil, plus the nice little extra touch of 'Coventry – England' at the bottom. A quality item, it demonstrated

With long wheelbase and the 4.0 litre AJ-V8 as standard, the Sovereign provides an extra dimension in space, luxury and performance.

Remarkably, the benefits of the long wheelbase have been gained without significant loss or change to any aspect of performance. Even the Sovereign's appearance is barely affected by its full five inches of extra length. Externally, this is absorbed into the rear doors and creates only a subtle increase in on-the-road presence. Internally, however, those additional inches make a significant difference. All the extra room is between the front and rear seats or, in more practical terms, where every inch creates legroom and working space for the rear passengers. To further increase space behind an unoccupied front passenger seat there is an electric control, located on the back of the seat, which enables it to be moved fully forward by driver or rear passengers.

Seats are in five-flute, hand-crafted leather with trim colour-keyed in the Classic theme in a choice of six colours. Wood veneers are in Burr Walnut. Numerous detailed features make a colour-keyed leather handbrake grip, thick-pile floor mats and veneer surrounds on the door switchpacks.

The Sovereign exterior is distinguished by the chrome on radiator grille vanes, door frames and rear lamp surrounds.

In addition to the three solid colours, metallic paint in a choice of 13 colours is standard. Wheels are Starburst alloys.

For those who desire the Sovereign's outstanding level of performance and equipment but without the long wheelbase, the Sovereign is available with short wheelbase.

Sovereign long wheelbase interior - Cobalt/Flax with Burr Walnut veneer

- 5149 mm long wheelbase
- 16 point colour option
- 7x16" Starburst alloy wheels
- touring suspension
- Three-position seat memory including steering wheel and mirror positions
- heated front and rear seats option
- mirror pack option incorporating electrochromic and power foldback door mirrors

SOVEREIGN - AN EXTRA DIMENSION

V8 XJ SERIES

attention to detail throughout, such as the 'D' emblem at the base of every page, the onion-skins back and front, watermarked backgrounds to pages, and – the finishing touch – royal warrants on the back cover, embossed in gold.

Another year and yet another new brochure set. Now with a green tinted cover showing an XJR at speed, the 2001 Jaguar issue had fewer pages and took on a slightly revised approach to its interior design. There were more superb studio images, superimposed onto arty – if a little contrived – backgrounds, such as the two-page spread of a stationary XJ8 4.0-litre with no driver but set against a motioned background!

An interesting marketing point here concerns this 4.0-litre model and the smaller-engined Sport. Launched as the 3.2-litre Sport, in 1999 the latter model was temporarily discontinued from the range. In the 2000 brochure the 4.0-litre had been upgraded to fill the gap and was presented, as the material proclaimed, with 'Sporting Refinement', with revised seating and exterior trim. Then in 2001, due to pressure from dealers, the 3.2-litre Sport was reinstated, and ironically – returning to an economic

practice going back to the XK120s – the brochure pictures for both cars were exactly the same! At the same time the 3.2-litre XJ8 was renamed the Executive, an allusion back to X-300 practice.

An attractive new feature was the colour and trim section at the rear of the brochure which not only showed the colour swatches but provided miniature images of each colour on a car. This approach was also adopted for Daimler and subsequently other model brochures, yet another example of moving forward in content, sophistication, and style.

If the 2000 Daimler brochure was impressive, the 2001 edition was more so, with a red hardbound cover with dust jacket. Now expanded to 36 pages (from 20), it is the epitome of quality and is another example worthy of mention alongside the best material. The inside front cover, for example, has a sepia image of a Daimler at speed on a suburban road. An onion-skin opens to reveal full car images shown in motion, and a beautiful full-page picture of a radiator grille being welded (a throwback to the Series 3 material discussed earlier).

ABOVE *Well laid out pages with excellent pictures of the interiors of each model showed more confidence in the XJ8 than in the previous six-cylinder cars.*

BELOW *Comparative pictures for the 2001 3.2-litre Sport and the 2000 4.0-litre XJ8. Apart from the background they are exactly the same!*

End of the line

Something entirely different came next, as later in 2001 Jaguar decided to change their whole literature design philosophy. Giant perfect-bound portrait format brochures measuring approximately 13½in x 9in (343mm x 229mm) were published for all models including the XJ8, with a new look, a new cover, and a colour scheme of silver and green – in fact nearly every car featured within was silver!

Performance was definitely the theme here, with most of the newly produced photography being of cars in motion. The layout approach used small and large photographs spread across pages or parts thereof with scant text. The brochure was obviously intended for global consumption as both left- and right-hand-drive examples are depicted. It was also the first brochure to feature a connection with the then relatively new Jaguar Formula One Racing Team.

This type of material was definitely 'lifestyle' oriented, with a single page devoted to technical information and eight pages of chequerboard-style small detail pictures of equipment and extras. This approach allowed prospective owners to browse and 'pick and choose' the specification (Habitat style). Surprisingly this material saw a return to a separate insert for exterior paint finishes.

This format of brochure was followed up slightly later in the year (the last year of XJ8 production) by a slimline version in card opening out to six pages. Of the same style, it depicted half frontal images of just the SE and Sport models, as everything else was being scaled down in production. The centre-page strapline read 'All good things – come to an end', confirming the end of the line. These final cars had enhanced specification and both sold at exactly the same price of £35,950.

BELOW *The two hardbound Daimler volumes from 2000 and 2001 – impressive material when one considers that fewer than 4,750 Daimlers were produced between 1997 and 2002!*

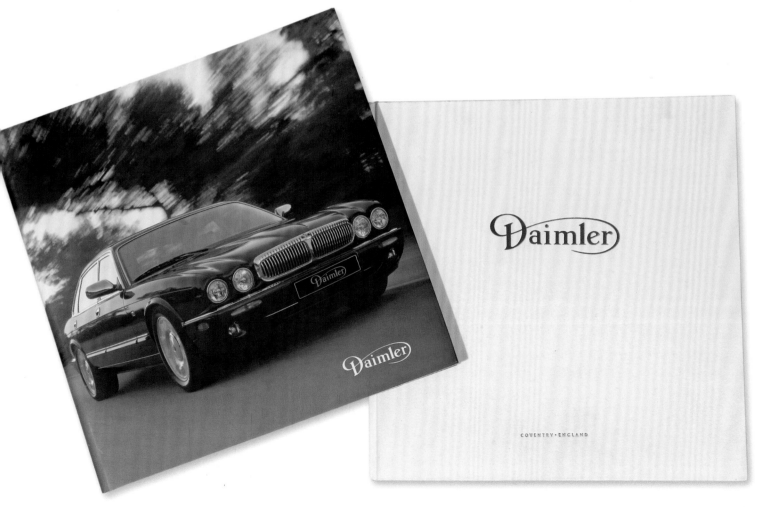

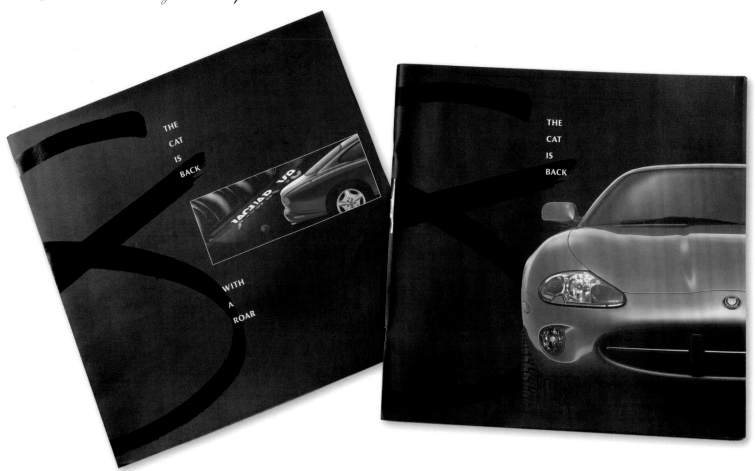

ABOVE *The strong black cover treatment with varnished '8' and an image of just part of the nose separated the style of the early XK8 material from anything else Jaguar had done up to that time.*

FAR RIGHT ABOVE
This superb triple-page studio picture in the launch brochure for the new XK8 measures nearly 3ft (0.9m) across.

FAR RIGHT BELOW
High tech stuff for the XK8 launch material. Here an onion-skin has been used to good effect: printed with the body, it opens up to reveal the exposed engine bay beneath.

In summary, the material published for the XJ8 was quite extensive and very well presented and produced. The 1990s proved that to keep abreast of an ever-changing market for prestige cars, the promotional material as well as the cars had to be regularly updated.

XK8 – The Cat is Back

The XK8 sports car (replacing the XJS) was introduced in 1996 and remained in production until 2005. It was a vitally important addition to the range, heralding extensive technical innovations and, as far as marketing was concerned, bringing back a more sporting image not seen since the E-type. As such it was entitled to be marketed in an appropriate manner. It is surprising, therefore, that much of the material produced followed the same pattern as that of the saloons.

'The Cat is Back' was the phrase adopted for the launch promotion, comprising a large, square, 50-page brochure and an abridged six-page folder. The quality of the brochure stood out, as was deserved for such an important new car. It was loaded with most of the features used

before, such as onion-skins, double- and triple-page fold-outs, diagrams, studio work, and location pictures, and nearly a third was given over to technical aspects and development of the new model. It was a really impressive item, and although very different in style to the early E-type material, it similarly emphasised the Grand Touring aspects of the car without reference to race-bred competition.

A new brochure appeared for 1998, back to the corporate style with a black cover and a green car. Within its 30 pages much was refined and amended from the earlier version, but there was also some new content and changes in colour schemes, etc.

With the launch of the XKR supercharged car in 1998 a separate, additional brochure was produced. With few pages, it concentrated on the changes and specification of the car, with just one page singing the praises of the new power unit and transmission. It did, however, incorporate some interesting features.

For 1999 the corporate cream cover was adopted for a new brochure incorporating the XKR model. The content was a revamp of the earlier black brochure, with many of the XKR

'Every effortless movement confirms the XK8 as the most perfectly evolved sporting Jaguar ever.'

Believed to have been photographed in Sardinia, this is one of six impressive colour spreads of the new XK8 on location that mostly portray it in lifestyle scenarios.

FAR BELOW RIGHT
A striking cover for the XKR, all in red to match its launch colour, with just the nose and the 'Supercharged' badge showing.

images taken from the same 'Grand Canyon' photo-shoot used for the launch material.

2000 saw another new brochure to corporate style, with the black nose section of an XK8 on the cover. With its new style of layout and a mix of enhanced studio photography, monotone moving images, and location shots, it portrays a very different approach to XK marketing.

Not resting on its laurels, another new style of brochure appeared in 2002, copying that which has already been described for the XJ8 of this period. It used a mixture of superbly photographed and printed pictures of the cars in motion or against lifestyle backdrops, the fact that all the vehicles used were non-UK registered presenting an air of internationalism. This move to evocative imagery was accompanied by a distinct lack of text, there being probably less than 200 words in the whole brochure.

Using the same format yet another new XK brochure appeared in 2003 that was even more

prestigious, with more pages, onion-skins again, and separated out into sections for spirit, soul, and body. By this time the XK market must have spoken for itself, because there were no lifestyle backdrops, merely high-key studio photography and cars depicted at speed. The first 34 pages were all pictures, with no text whatsoever, while further on much emphasis was placed on new interior trim and styles – hence there were no less than two pages at the back showing every variant! For some reason, however, a paint chart was still a separate item.

This was a striking brochure and one that was followed through for the X-type and S-type models, but it was short-lived. It reappeared slightly later in a slimline abridged version – this time including an integrated colour chart!

It is fair to assume that the dealers did not like this style of larger brochure because of its sheer size: it was awkward to display and awkward for prospective customers to handle and carry.

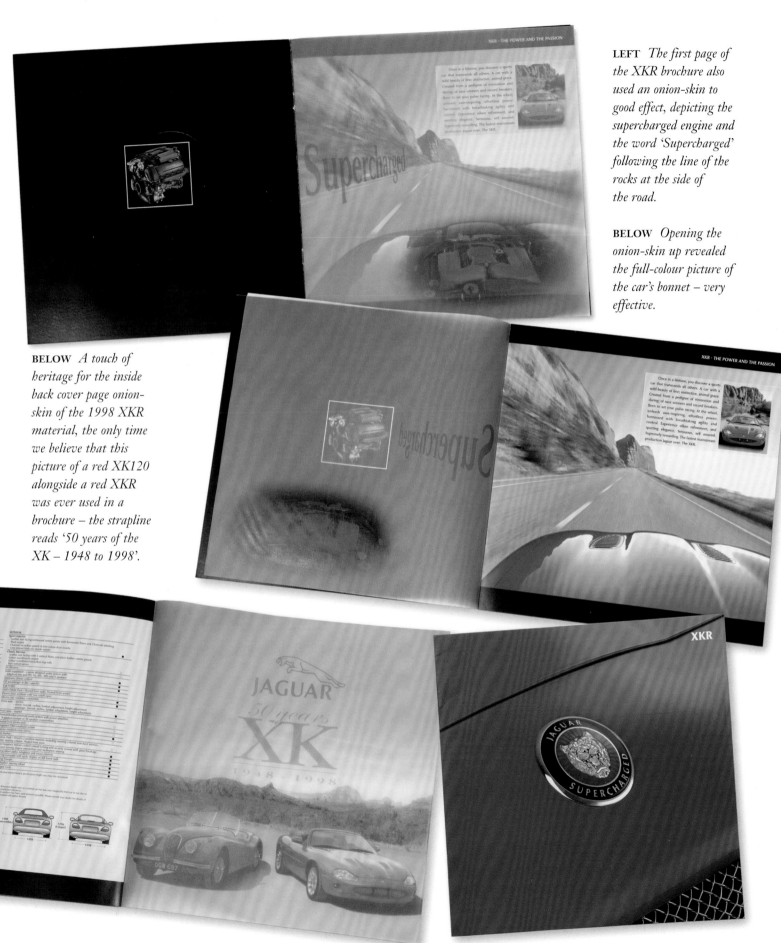

LEFT *The first page of the XKR brochure also used an onion-skin to good effect, depicting the supercharged engine and the word 'Supercharged' following the line of the rocks at the side of the road.*

BELOW *Opening the onion-skin up revealed the full-colour picture of the car's bonnet – very effective.*

BELOW *A touch of heritage for the inside back cover page onion-skin of the 1998 XKR material, the only time we believe that this picture of a red XK120 alongside a red XKR was ever used in a brochure – the strapline reads '50 years of the XK – 1948 to 1998'.*

An example of the great, moody, monotone imagery used in the 2000 XK brochure.

There are two points to note here. Firstly, this stunning spread captures perfectly the curvaceous nature of the XK; and secondly, despite the fact that this brochure is for UK consumption, all the picture captions are in seven languages!

An interesting spread from one of the US brochures depicts the XK8 alongside an archive image of Mike Hawthorn in a Jaguar D-type at Le Mans.

FAR RIGHT, TOP LEFT Taken from the 2002 XK brochure, this is the first time all four models were featured in this way, providing clear comparisons of trim, alloy wheel type, and colour.

FAR RIGHT, TOP RIGHT The new house style of large, portrait-format, perfect-bound brochure for XKs in 2002, 60 pages in length.

ABOVE *Typical example of the high-key studio photography used for this XK brochure.*

RIGHT *Emphasis is placed on the later interior trim options for the XK.*

BELOW *Revised front cover treatment for 2005 included a matching sleeve and, a first, the provision of a full price list and specification booklet to match.*

FAR RIGHT, TOP *A really nice feature of the last XK brochure was the inclusion of side views of the car in all the available colour schemes and alloy wheel combinations.*

In addition Jaguar must have found them expensive to produce, which is probably why the format changed yet again, back to a smaller landscape style, in 2004/5.

The first offering was still a quality item printed on satin paper and 50 pages in length. The interior was also revised, with a return to text on every page (although not a lot of it), with quite flowery reports on 'To Own a Jaguar', 'To Drive an XK', etc. Most of the photography was again new but other information was a direct lift from the earlier material. It represented a welcome return to a brochure that was useful to a potential purchaser rather than something from a lifestyle magazine with little real 'meat' in it.

2005 saw another new brochure, with a stylised though highly detailed image of a black XKR on the cover. This brochure even came within its own sleeve. Changes in the models meant all-new pictures, some digitally enhanced, and the layout was a logical extension of what had been developing since 2003. This was effectively the last of the standard model brochures for the XK8 and XKR.

Special editions

The extensive material on the XK also includes special edition folders, starting in 2000 with the Silverstone model to commemorate Jaguar's entry into Formula 1 and the first UK race at the circuit of the same name.

For the US market small brochures were produced for their equivalent of the Carbon Fibre model plus their unique Portfolio cars.

We should also mention the commemorative '100' models produced in both XKR and XJR forms to celebrate the 100th anniversary of Sir William Lyons, the founder of the company. Just 500 cars were produced, all in black, promoted with a large portrait-style folder and separate information sheets on the cars. Jaguar's marketing policy here is difficult to understand compared to more exotic material like that for the Carbon Fibre and other special editions.

Coming to the end of XK production, for 2005 Jaguar announced the final model, known as the 4.2 S in the UK/European market and
the Victory in the US. This fully equipped model came in both XK8 and XKR forms, and another unique brochure was produced to promote it. This was hardbound, with a white cover with simple foil blocking and an onion-skin style sleeve with foil seal – a very high quality publication which seemed a little over-the-top for a car that was very shortly to be deleted from the range.

ABOVE *The marketing approach for the XKR Silverstone followed more of a press pack theme, with individual sheets of information tucked behind a die-cut image of the car within a folder.*

ABOVE *The 2004 XKR 400 special edition. In contrast to the Silverstone, this was a substantial 28-page brochure within a silver protective cover, a black sleeve, and an envelope! A unique item, and very attractive and substantial for a limited edition.*

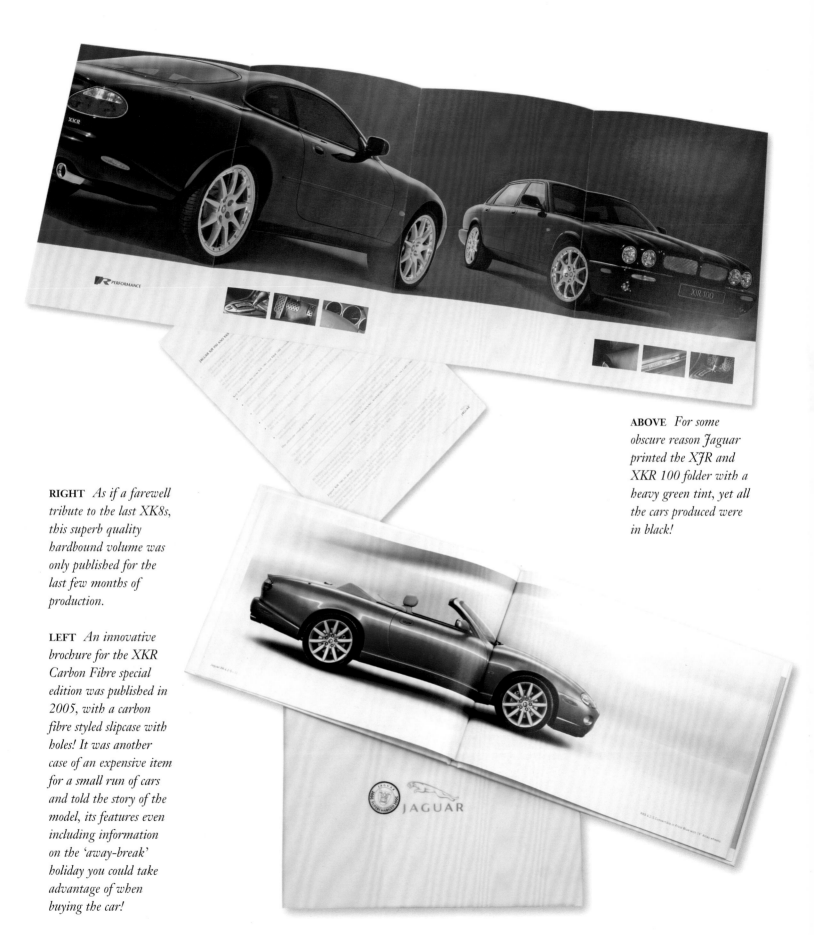

ABOVE *For some obscure reason Jaguar printed the XJR and XKR 100 folder with a heavy green tint, yet all the cars produced were in black!*

RIGHT *As if a farewell tribute to the last XK8s, this superb quality hardbound volume was only published for the last few months of production.*

LEFT *An innovative brochure for the XKR Carbon Fibre special edition was published in 2005, with a carbon fibre styled slipcase with holes! It was another case of an expensive item for a small run of cars and told the story of the model, its features even including information on the 'away-break' holiday you could take advantage of when buying the car!*

167

A new vision

In this final chapter we look closely at Jaguar's marketing plans for the entirely new range of cars that would take them into the next millennium: the medium sized S-type; an entirely new 'baby' Jaguar; and all-new technology for the next generation XK and XJ.

The introduction of the S-type model resulted in a wider-based model range for 1999 and saw a return to the core values of the late 1950s and 1960s in marketing terms. It was a car that was to echo the fortunes of the famous Mark 2, but in a far more competitive market!

Very little information about the new Jaguar had been drip-fed to the general public, but in June 1999 the first promotional literature was released (before the launch) in the form of an A4 eight-page folder in colour containing images that would become very popular during the first year of production. As had happened many times before, because this was prepared in advance it was later reprinted with more accurate information.

Jaguar were looking to capture new customers with this car, so the launch brochure was naturally impressive. Packed with information

on a mix of textured matt and art paper, a turnabout was the inclusion of all the technical and development information at the back of the brochure, nevertheless impressively dealt with in ten pages and with full-page colour pictures. Following a practice adopted earlier, phrases of technical interest were published in eight languages.

There were only three models available at this time, which were hardly distinguishable from the outside, yet Jaguar chose to impress potential customers by publishing no less than six two-page colour spreads of the car! Another interesting aspect is that the brochure portrayed this as a family car, with the emphasis on enjoyment and holidays, even if some of the pictures (like the little girl peacefully asleep on the back seat) were rather understated in black and white.

This brochure was reprinted for the following year with most of the content intact, but was reduced slightly in size and the textured pages were replaced. Some interior pictures were also re-photographed to reflect changes (there was no retouching now), and some were moved to aid the printing.

In 2001 the brochure format reverted to the house style with a green cover. This approach introduced a proper 'contents' page and all-location shots of the car, with studio shots for the interiors. Imaginative positive to negative photography was also employed, and although there seemed less emphasis on the family aspects there were still water-marked full-page images of the family playing football, and oh yes, the little girl peacefully asleep in the car reappeared, now full-page but rendered in monotone.

By this time Jaguar had dropped the use of Nikasil linings for the V8 engines, so no mention was made of this material, something that had been considered quite advanced and a benefit in the earlier brochure but was by now regarded as an embarrassment!

A smaller version of this brochure, apparently to be unique to the S-type, was produced later that year. This was of only 22 pages.

Also later that year an additional model was launched, the S-type Sport, and to avoid the cost of reprinting the full brochure a six-page card folder was produced.

The next full brochure in 2002 took on the 'corporate' style mentioned previously of a portrait-format, oversized offering. Perhaps Jaguar had now come to terms with the fact that many S-type owners were existing customers downsizing from an XJ or moving back to the Jaguar marque – hence this brochure echoed the theme of the other models, now with more lifestyle imagery rather than family involvement.

Later that year a 'preview' 20-page interim brochure was produced and sent out to dealers for distribution in readiness for model changes. From this Jaguar then produced a further portrait-format brochure for the new S-type, now with a new cover. This was expanded to

ABOVE _Although not the prettiest of Jaguar dashboards, it was felt to be so new that it deserved excellent coverage._

RIGHT *A change of brochure size, a move to art paper, and the use of colour images in place of muddy black and white for greater emphasis.*

BELOW *Photography and printing quality made the early S-type material very impressive and enticing for prospective buyers.*

ABOVE *Another new feature for 2001 was this excellent display of miniature car images to show off the exterior paint schemes.*

TOP *For the 2001 brochure negative imagery was employed to good effect.*

cover the then new 2.5-litre and 4.2-litre models. Out went people and lifestyle and in came cars depicted in motion. The S-type fared better than all the other models with yet another new brochure and a smaller-sized version for 2003, with the most striking of all front covers and now covering the facelifted models in full detail.

After the launch of the 2.7-litre Diesel S-type with a simple folder as an interim measure, the S-type material followed suit with the rest of the marque and the more conventional look to the front cover (see the XJ section later in this chapter).

For 2005 the style of brochure changed yet again to the new corporate look of a landscape format with a black cover. Great play was made of the interior, to which seven pages were devoted, but it seemed as if Jaguar didn't have full confidence in the new alloy dash treatment as it received less prominence than the conventional style.

The X-type

The X-type provided Jaguar with a unique opportunity to enter a market dominated by established models like the Audi A4 and BMW

RIGHT *Despite the 2003 S-type brochure following corporate style, the front cover was certainly the most striking of them all.*

ENJOY YOUR REWARD

S-TYPE INTERIORS

ABOVE TOP *From the 2005 'black' brochure, this picture of the alloy dashboard model with two-colour trim isn't shown with the same confidence as…*

ABOVE *…the more attractive image of the walnut veneered version from the same brochure.*

LEFT *The S-type Sport model used cheaper 'pick up' literature to support its launch, and the same approach has since been followed to promote the Sports Collection equipment and the XS and Plus special editions.*

RIGHT *Launch treatment for the S-type Diesel. Folders like this provide the opportunity for early promotion of new models without the need to print complete brochures.*

3 Series. The strategy of this 'New Generation Jag' image didn't quite come off because the styling of the car was too like the 'old man's' XJ, and even the promotional material wasn't modern enough to capture a younger audience.

Things got off to a good start with a new policy of pre-launch enticement, more so than with the S-type. The then Director of UK Operations, Andrew Lester, with the aid of the dealers, sent out an introductory pack with letter to prospective customers, comprising a 'Priority Information Request' postcard, a detailed price list, a standard options and equipment list, and a 14-page full-colour brochure about the car, printed in no less than

seven languages for global consumption. If that wasn't enough, at the rear there was a pocket containing a CD which provided a download for a website providing a useful and youthful organiser. A bespoke website was also built for the car.

Instead of following this through with more such striking and 'youthful' material, Jaguar opted to follow the corporate line thereafter and produced a large portrait-style brochure for 2002, which was later reprinted to take account of the then new 2.0-litre models.

For 2003 there was another new brochure, which, again following the style of the day, lacked some of the impact of the previous year's

material. Out went lifestyle, people, and the Habitat approach to equipment levels, back came the normal layout and pictures you'd have found in brochures produced for any other Jaguar model of the time.

With the arrival of the 2.0-litre Diesel X-type the launch information took the form of a simple folder like that produced for the S-type, and similar treatment was given to the first Estate models.

2004 saw more new material that again followed the standard Jaguar revised format of a landscape, silver car approach. This was followed in 2005 by the 'black' theme, this year's brochure being later reprinted to accommodate

the X-type S model (although merely by the change of one colour spread), while the picture of the Sport became the Sport Premium, another picture became the Sovereign, and there were similar changes to the text and specifications.

The same style was followed for the unique Estate car brochure, a lavish approach for effectively one model that clearly showed the importance that Jaguar placed in it (the only production estate car the company has ever manufactured). This has been joined by another unique brochure, for the 2.2-litre Diesel models (saloon and estate in the one publication), which has also taken the corporate style of cover.

ABOVE *The 'preview' pack issued by dealers to selected prospective customers.*

RIGHT *Some of the 2002 X-type brochure content tried to reflect the younger customers the company anticipated would buy the car.*

ABOVE *Another lifestyle page from the X-type brochure.*

RIGHT *X-type brochure or Habitat catalogue? Taken from the 2002 X-type material, this idea of picking and choosing your specification by picture was also used in other Jaguar material but was much more effective for this model.*

BELOW *Other X-type material has varied from a brochure for the X-type S through to postcard literature for the Getaway equipment pack and Sports*

Collection body kits, and – best of all – an intelligently put together high-gloss folder on the Spirit limited edition entitled 'Improve Your Body Language'.

BOTTOM *Typical of later brochure treatment for Jaguar was the inclusion of side panel information*

with comments from the technical personnel involved with the cars.

RIGHT *Later X-type Diesel material finally brought the saloons and estate cars together into one brochure.*

CENTRE and **BOTTOM** *An extravagant brochure was created for the X-type Indianapolis model, with an alcantara-finished dust cover and printed on superb high-gloss board for maximum effect – a really over-the-top quality item to a high standard of contemporary design. If only all the X-type material could have been produced with such flair!*

Although the X-type has been quite a successful model for Jaguar in many ways it hasn't achieved its aim of bringing down the average customer age significantly, in part, perhaps, due to a lack of the vibrancy that this type of market demands.

The new XJ

The replacement XJ, codenamed X-350, would inevitably cater for the more traditional Jaguar buyer, hence despite its new technology, the styling and promotional material would have to be geared to the upper-middle class level of customer.

Prior to the launch a lot of effort was put into the marketing of the new car. For example, it was featured on their website and the press had the opportunity to drive and report on the car prior to its launch in 2003. In September 2002 the marketing department, via the dealers, sent out a box to prospective customers with a personal letter from Mike Beasley, then Managing Director of Jaguar Cars. Within the card box was a 28-page brochure within a sleeve, headed 'The New XJ – A Leap Ahead – Preview'.

ABOVE *Another pre-launch package. Nice, if a little bland for such a luxurious new car as the XJ.*

BELOW *An interesting comparison of the launch brochure for the all-aluminium XJ with the equivalent Audi A8 and BMW 7 Series presentations. The Audi boasted an alloy sub-structure emphasised by the aluminium brochure sleeve and the bright plaque reading 'It's taken Audi twelve years to build one car'. BMW's offering had nearly twice the number of pages of the Jag publication, with some excellent photography.*

This was followed by another mail-out, more suited to the business community, of a glossy card birthday folder with a black XJ set against a black background and the simple words 'Now pure self-indulgence makes good business sense'. This included some interesting comparison figures between the XJ6 and the Mercedes S280 and S220CDi, and of the XJ8 4.2 compared to the BMW 745i and Mercedes S Class S430.

The first XJ brochure came out for the launch in 2003 in the usual format. The two-tone cover was unique to the model if uninspiring. Out of 66 pages, 16 were devoted to excellent photographs of the car but with no text at all and a further ten pages to the car's technical prowess.

Although a quality item it was still lacklustre by previous standards, being best described as a little too clinically clean. Reprinted the following year it moved back to the 'black' cover style of the other cars, while internally, although the same as the earlier printing, the backgrounds and layout were improved for better appeal.

The next printing had the same cover style as other 2005 Jaguar brochures, but also included the newer long wheelbase models and had new photographs inside.

For the introduction of the 2.7-litre Diesel XJ6 Jaguar adopted the by now normal treatment of issuing an interim card folder with just enough information and some enticing photographs, but no detail specification of the diesel aspect.

For 2006 there was yet another new full-sized landscape brochure in the new style, featuring a car against a semi-surreal sky background. This represents the best XJ brochure so far, with new creative photography. The whole emphasis is on quality and image and it is very informative, as is deserved for the flagship of the range.

A new Daimler derivative was launched as an addition to the range and this received individual prestige treatment, much as the previous Daimler models had, in the form of a bonded leather hardbound book in a leather sleeve.

ABOVE *A good example of the change in photography style and layout: the first and third generation XJ brochures.*

LEFT *The changing face of all-aluminium XJ promotional material since 2003.*

The Jaguar XJ range

XJ EXECUTIVE

The 3.0 litre V6 model is generously equipped: a six-speed electronic automatic transmission, air-damped CATS Computer Active Technology Suspension, Dynamic Stability Control (DSC) and Adaptive Restraint Technology System (A.R.T.S.) are amongst its many standard features.

XJ SPORT PREMIUM

For the enthusiast who revels in sports car responsiveness, the Sport Premium provides greater feel and control through firmer spring and damper settings. The Sport Premium is distinguished by body coloured features and a mesh grille insert.

XJ SOVEREIGN

The lavishly equipped Sovereign adds to the Executive specification with 16-way electric front seats, soft grain leather, JaguarVoice, satellite navigation, Bluetooth™ telephone connectivity, Bi-xenon headlights, Rapier 18" wheels and the exclusive Sovereign badge.

XJR

The ultimate performance XJ with its racing-inspired mesh grille, Sabre 19" wheels and famous R badges. The hugely powerful supercharged 4.2 litre V8 is well matched by R Performance brakes and a chassis that's firm yet smooth-riding.

XJ SUPER V8

Indulgent luxury blends with lavish equipment in the Super V8, which includes Adaptive Cruise Control (ACC), front parking assist, DVD player, rear multimedia controls, 4-zone automatic air conditioning, R Performance brakes and Rapier 18" wheels amongst its standard features. Behind the chrome surround grille with its bright mesh is a legendary supercharged 4.2 litre V8.

THE NEW
XK

Expression

from
HATFIELDS JAGUAR

Gorgeous is delighted to meet you.

DRAMATICALLY BEAUTIFUL, with state-of-the-art technology and a luxurious interior: the all-new XK coupé and convertible will soon be here. The most advanced Jaguar ever effortlessly blends the refinement of a Grand Tourer with the thrilling performance and dynamics of a real sports car. Look inside and get to know the new XK - and some of our other cars - a little bit better.

JAGUAR

ABOVE *A good point of reference for a potential XJ buyer is this spread showing what the various models look like, with accompanying explanation.*

RIGHT *Brochure material produced by the new advertising agency at Jaguar for the aluminium XK sports car.*

The All New XK

Coded X-150, the 'All New XK', as Jaguar calls it, was launched in March 2006, replacing the XK8. This marked an important change for Jaguar, with a move to a new PR company, Euro RSCG/Fuel being appointed their worldwide advertising agency.

Following a major review Jaguar wanted to re-focus their marketing position, particularly in view of the new XK sports car and other new models to be released. The early fruits of their collaboration with Euro RSCG/Fuel can be seen below.

Careful pre-launch release of the new car included a return to television advertising, reflecting the style that the new advertising agency has created in the brochure material – based very much on aspirational aspects, the 'Gorgeous' theme, and less specific detail on the actual car.

The first brochure was somewhat of a surprise, therefore, and was released pre-launch in mid-2005. This returned to an extra-large size – 11½in x 14in (292mm x 356mm) – and was very much a teaser, with little text, big pictures, and no prices or specifications, but it

LEFT *Typical example of the design for the 2006 XK brochure.*

LEFT *Sample spreads from both the early XK brochures concentrate on its aspirational appeal.*

TOP RIGHT *Looks familiar – compare to the cover of the early XJ-S brochure on page 103.*

BELOW RIGHT
Unusual yet impressive vertical spreads mix well…

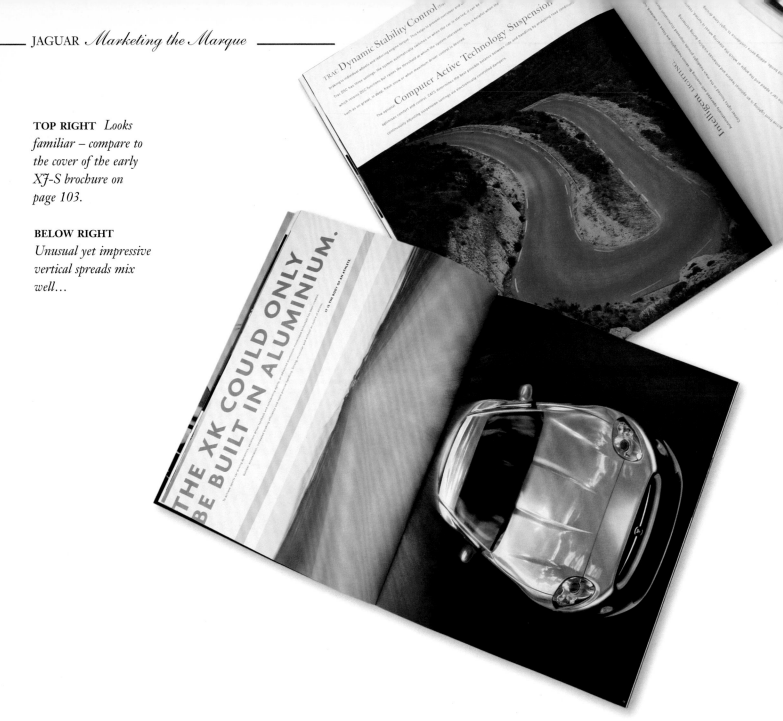

did include colour schemes and alloy wheel choices. It all looked impressive, certainly in terms of size and extent (28 pages), but the style and layout was something very different and unfortunately the matt paper didn't show off the photographs to their best advantage. This brochure was also produced in a smaller size.

For the launch of the car a new and more substantial brochure was produced, of 62 pages with a simple front and rear cover treatment and packed full of photographs of the actual cars. Its very contemporary, attractive layout included some interesting features not used by Jaguar before, plus a couple that take us back to earlier chapters!

Conclusions

This journey into Jaguar marketing has taken us through more than 75 years, from a time when the company was desperately trying to establish the marque, through the launch of the Jaguar name and the expansion period of the 1950s and 1960s, and from there to public and back to private ownership before finally entering the Ford era and witnessing the dramatic recent changes in its model range. It is a fascinating history that very few other manufacturers could match. The whole history of the company and its cars is well reflected in the promotional material it has produced.

Index